PARTIES AND POLITICS
IN CONTEMPORARY JAPAN

ROBERT A. SCALAPINO

AND JUNNOSUKE MASUMI

PARTIES AND

POLITICS IN

CONTEMPORARY

Japan

UNIVERSITY OF CALIFORNIA PRESS

BERKELEY and LOS ANGELES

1964

University of California Press

Berkeley and Los Angeles, California

Cambridge University Press

London, England

© 1962 by The Regents of the University of California

Library of Congress Catalog Card Number: 61–14279

Designed by Frank J. Lieberman

Printed in the United States of America

Second Printing, 1964

PREFACE

Much has been written in recent years about the study of comparative politics. To a considerable extent, this new writing stems from the discovery of the non-Western world by Western social scientists. In the future, no doubt, our pioneer voyages of today will be considered just as primitive as the voyage of Columbus to the "new world" five centuries ago. Fortunately, however, we can hope for rapid progress. The social scientists of Asia are now prepared to join with their counterparts in the West in the use of new data, techniques, and ideas.

This is a period when we need the widest possible exploration, using various combinations of methods and disciplines. It is our conviction that the science of comparative politics can best be advanced at this point by the development of empirical studies in depth, studies that seek to improve the techniques for the analysis of the political structure and process in a given society or culture, subsociety or subculture. Only when we have a number of such studies can we approach comparative politics with both precision and subtlety. Our purpose in this brief volume is to experiment with the union of several methods in an effort to shed new light upon selective aspects of political organization and procedure in contemporary Japan. We have sought to combine a historical approach with certain social science techniques for purposes of establishing our basic hypotheses. Then we have attempted to test and illustrate these hypotheses by using a specific case study, in this instance the May–June incidents of 1960.

We have begun with the historical approach, because through this we hope to convey some flavor of the cultural background out of which modern Japan has emerged, and the cultural context in which the operations of Japanese politics take place. Perhaps we should make clear our use of the term "culture." We do not see culture as a static, organic, monolithic force. To us, culture is the product of an infinitely complex combination of forces, constantly in flux and to some extent in conflict, but wherein the dominant or uniform traits of any given moment serve as major determinants of the attitudes and actions of various human groups. Culture must encompass in some measure the totality of the society, both the dominant and the conflicting forces of value, organization, and behavior, both the indigenous and the foreign elements that influence a way of life. In using the concept of culture, the political scientist must think in dynamic terms and in terms of a balance of forces. Although no one will ever be able to analyze completely the chemical composition, as it were, of a given culture at a given time, the importance of quantification is implicit in our usage of this concept. Unless culture lends itself to the realities of social change as well as of dominant traits, unless it can encompass the elements of paradox, conflict, and confusion as well as those of symmetry, interrelation, and progression, it is of scant use to the political scientist.

Accepting these ideas, we can use the historical approach effectively to discern in general terms the type and amount of change that has characterized the evolution of modern Japanese politics since the Meiji era. Change is meaningful only when it is viewed against continuity, of course. Nor do these two concepts lie in total contradistinction. Change in any society is mainly the product of the gradual infusion of limited new elements into a situation where old ones continue to exist. Rarely is there a battle to the death, a preordained commitment to exclusiveness. As the new infiltrates the old, the old influences the new. Japan is a magnificent example of this fact. Adaptation and fusion have been far more common characteristics than obliteration.

In discussing political or social change, two factors assume great importance. One is timing; the other is resources. Ours is a world in which there has occurred an increasing universalization of basic values. The historians of future generations will probably find this fact the most significant single development of the 20th century. In the zenith period of Western imperialism, values that had once been largely confined to a narrow rim of western Europe and the United States, values that had developed indigenously out of the evolution of these societies, suddenly acquired a universal appeal, at least in terms of the dominant elites. What are these values? Perhaps they can be summarized briefly in four words: progress, industrialization, science, and democracy. Who does not want these things today? The significant thing about our conflict with the Communists in the light of history may be not our differences, but the fact that we both covet the same ends; we both struggle for the right to be called progressive, industrialized, scientific, and democratic.

For this reason, the point in history at which a society enters the "modernization stream," or the point at which it emerges into the universalist, world channel, is of supreme importance. The nature and interrelation of economic, social, and political structure-processes will be profoundly affected. In these respects, it is much more logical to compare Japan with Germany— or even the Soviet Union—than with Great Britain or the United States, or, indeed, with much of Asia. The composite global knowledge of and experience with economic-political techniques at the particular time when a society enters the modernization stream, the prevailing world values and "waves of the future"— all are critically important factors in determining the tempo, structure, and processes that will characterize that society. We are now well aware of the fact that a given economic stage does not produce a given set of political institutions and processes—indeed, that 20th-century economic stages are not the same as those of the 18th and 19th centuries in terms of some of their most basic characteristics. This is what makes the non-Western world significantly different from the so-called "advanced Western societies," in addition to the differences in cultural background.

Resources are a much more conventional element in connection with comparative politics, but, nonetheless, an element of deep and continuing significance. Location, topography, climate, size of area, natural and human resources—all are involved in our concept of resources. Certainly, this element has become more subject to control or compensation with the advance of science. Still, it provides definite limits or boundaries to political expression, directly or indirectly. In the case of most societies, resources used in this broad sense provide the critical limits or opportunities.

Having sought to deal with the above factors, at least by implication, in the historical background, we have then proceeded to attempt some quantification of a few specific, selected political elements of contemporary Japanese society. At every point, we have attempted to interrelate structure and process. In our opinion, it is impossible to separate them, and productive of error to attempt to do so. Political and social structure are closely tied, as we have attempted to show; the one is reflective of the other, and both can be understood only in terms of a fairly basic analysis of the political process, especially in view of the extensive fluidity that currently marks Japanese society. In this particular study, we have confined our interest to an attempt to measure the socioeconomic composition of the Japanese party elite, the relative importance of interest groups in connection with party structure and organization, and the elements affecting Japanese voting behavior at present. We are very much aware of the impossibility of precise measurements. We shall be content if the basic trends set forth in this work are correct, and if the composite method we have used has some merit for similar studies relating to other non-Western societies.

Finally, we wish to make it clear that we were not interested, here, in presenting a detailed, definitive study of the May–June incidents of 1960. We were interested in these incidents only as a case study relating to the hypotheses advanced earlier. Consequently, we have dealt with only those aspects of the inci-

Preface

dents that seemed germane to our interests, and only to the extent necessary to make our points.

As is always true, we are indebted to a number of people in connection with this manuscript. First, we should like to thank the Rockefeller Foundation, and especially Dr. Kenneth W. Thompson, for making this research possible. We should also like to express our appreciation to such colleagues as Ardath Burks, Nobutaka Ike, John Maki, David Sissons, and Robert Ward for helpful advice and suggestions. Since the manuscript was written in the United States, it was submitted to American scholars, but we are both deeply indebted to a large number of Japanese scholars for aid—past, present, and, we hope, future. We are also greatly appreciative of the labors of Mikio Higa, who compiled many of the statistics used in this study and prepared the index in our absence. We alone are responsible for the final product, but those mentioned above, together with our students and the members of the Center for Japanese Studies at Berkeley, have been extremely generous in reading and criticizing the original manuscript.

June, 1961   ROBERT A. SCALAPINO
                                            JUNNOSUKE MASUMI

CONTENTS

INTRODUCTION

Japan recently experienced the greatest mass movement in her political history. Thirteen million people signed petitions requesting dissolution of the House of Representatives and the holding of new elections. Six million workers supported these efforts with work stoppages. Hundreds of thousands of Japanese citizens, many of them completely new to political activities, demonstrated in Tokyo streets and around the Diet building. No Japanese political movement of the past has equaled this in terms of mass participation and sustained activity. Its leadership, its tactics, and the broad causative forces that created it are likely to be the subjects of intensive analysis for the indefinite future.

The immediate issues in this crisis were the revised United States–Japan Security Treaty and the methods used by the Kishi government in obtaining its passage. But underlying these issues were others that pertained to the whole nature of Japanese politics in theory and in practice. This was the type of episode which, fully analyzed, might lay bare the very roots of the Japanese political process.

Will the May 19 incident and its aftermath achieve for Japan the symbolism achieved by the May 4 movement in

China? Certainly, many Japanese writers have tried to give it such connotations. The majority, however, have regarded it in a less sensational light as one of the many milestones in the political evolution of modern Japan, an event that will not acquire great historic significance in and of itself, but one that is reflective of the new sociopolitical forces now operative in Japan, forces that make this a truly transitional period. We still stand too close to the event to determine which of these two positions will ultimately be proven correct, although the latter position now seems closer to the facts. Nevertheless, it remains true that this crisis represented the most significant internal upheaval in Japan since the February 26 incident of 1936.

At the height of the May–June incident, it was frequently said that the whole future of Japanese democracy was at stake. What people meant by this varied greatly. The supporters of Mr. Kishi emphasized points entirely different from those raised by his opponents. In any case, such a statement is overly dramatic. The treaty crisis was a revelation more than a revolution. But this does not reduce its importance. Above all, it threw a strong spotlight upon the changing character of Japanese politics and the continuing weaknesses of Japanese democracy.

This is, therefore, an appropriate time to reappraise the political institutions and mores of Japan. In doing so, we intend to utilize several techniques. We shall begin with a brief historical survey. Our purpose here is threefold: to sketch with broad strokes the cultural background against which Japanese politics must be seen; to emphasize the particular timing of Japanese modernization, with its signal importance to every facet of the country's society; and to establish the necessity of viewing Japanese politics as a developmental process. Then we shall focus upon the contemporary political scene. Here, we shall utilize available social science techniques in examining data that pertains to political leadership, party organization, interest groups, and political behavior. Our aim will be to establish certain hypotheses about the Japanese political process. Finally, we shall use the May–June incident of 1960 as a case study against which to test these hypotheses.

I

THE BACKGROUND

The treaty crisis raised many questions. Some of these were simple, or at least obvious ones. Why did the Kishi cabinet have to resign when its party, the Liberal Democratic party, commanded an overwhelming majority in both houses of the Japanese Diet? Why did many of the Liberal Democratic leaders desert Kishi in his hour of need despite the fact that they had no significant differences with him over policy or even procedure? Why did the Socialists place such heavy emphasis upon unparliamentary and extra-parliamentary activities? Why did the general movement from the Diet to the streets occur so easily? Why did so many Japanese intellectuals participate directly in a political movement for the first time in history and regard their participation primarily as a struggle to preserve democracy against the "tyranny of the majority"? And, finally, why did the Japanese people seem reluctant to give the palm of victory to either side, showing instead a tendency to adopt a "plague on both your houses" attitude?

Behind these questions lie others that are less obvious in terms of the immediate events, but more fundamental. How should one define and classify the Japanese party system today? What forces—social, economic, and political—dominate the heights of Japanese politics, and what is their relative strength? What is the status of public participation in Japanese politics? And, lastly, what ideologies of politics, more specifically, of democracy, are current in modern Japan?

There are no easy answers to these questions. We propose here merely to advance certain hypotheses, based essentially upon an examination of contemporary Japanese parties. Let us first dip briefly into Japanese history.[1] The Japanese party movement was a truly hybrid product, formed from the union of indigenous, traditional forces with multiple Western stimuli. Both the idea and the ideology of the modern parties came largely from the West, but their organizational structure and mode of operation reflected heavily the Japanese scene—past and present.

The idea of political parties on the Western model first came to Japan in the period around 1872, nearly two decades before parliamentary government was effected. Thus Japanese parties operated for a considerable period, at least sporadically, without an institutional context. This was but one example of the curious impact of Western politics upon the Japanese scene. It was possible to borrow the latest Western fashions in constitutionalism, parliaments, and parties, but sometimes these came out of phase and with a bewildering rapidity that bore scant relation to internal social readiness. This inevitably affected these new forces in every conceivable

[1] For the background of the Japanese party movement, in English, see Nobutaka Ike, *The Beginnings of Political Democracy in Japan* (Baltimore, 1950); Harold Quigley, *Japanese Government and Politics* (New York, 1933); and Robert A. Scalapino, *Democracy and the Party Movement in Prewar Japan* (Berkeley and Los Angeles, 1953).

In Japanese, see Horie Eiichi and Tōyama Shigeki (eds.), *Jiyūminken ki no kenkyū* ("Studies on the Civil Rights Era") (4 vols.; Tokyo, 1959–60); *Meiji ishin shi kenkyū kōza* ("Historical Research Series on the Meiji Restoration") (6 vols.; Tokyo, 1958–59); *Meiji shi kenkyū sōsho* ("Research Series on Meiji History") (10 vols.; Tokyo, 1957–59); Shinobu Seisaburō, *Taishō demokurashi shi* ("History of Taishō Democracy") (3 vols.; Tokyo, 1954–59); Tōyama Shigeki, Imai Seiichi, and Fujiwara Akira, *Shōwa shi* ("History of Shōwa") (rev. ed.; Tokyo, 1959); and Ishida Takeshi, *Kindai Nihon seiji kōzō no kenkyū* ("Studies on the Political Structure of Modern Japan") (Tokyo, 1956).

respect, from their *raison d'être* and their image in the Japanese mind to their modes of operation. And as institutions were borrowed, so were ideas. From men like John Stuart Mill, Rousseau, Burke, Bluntschli, and many others came the ideas of liberty, progress, political competition, and majoritarianism, albeit with different emphases and approaches. Thus the early Meiji dissidents grasped both the *idea* of parties as potent weapons of peaceful opposition (in a period when military opposition was becoming increasingly difficult) and the *ideology* of liberalism as derived from Western experience.

But the central difficulties have already been suggested. The great historic problem of modern Japanese politics has been the high degree of separation between those formal political institutions borrowed from the West, together with the set of ideas that accompanied them, and the much broader social institutions bred from within Japanese society, together with the set of ideas that accompanied these. The latter forces were certainly influenced and affected by Westernism—in ever greater degree. But the timing and extent of that effect, and the very fact that they had a deeply rooted indigenous base spelled out the fundamental difference between them and such overseas imports as the National Diet and the political parties.

Thus the Diet and the parties have remained some·what foreign to the Japanese people. It cannot be denied, of course, that indigenous procedures have penetrated these institutions in many ways. Some of these procedures, indeed, have made their own contributions to the estrangement of the Japanese people from politics. The fact that the parties are essentially closed societies, mutual aid organizations of politicians in the manner of exclusive clubs, is more a product of Japanese "feudalism" than of the modern West. Nevertheless, such an institution as the Diet is sufficiently Western in its concept to demand rules drawn from that context if it is to bear any relation in function to its name. There is a certain premium upon direct debate, for instance, and the capacity to communicate with the opposition; hence there is the necessity to protect minority rights and accept majority decisions. Without these principles, no democratic parliament can

The Background

function. And yet, in Japan, the historic principles of organization and decision making were different: not direct debate, but indirect negotiation; not communication with the opposition, but aloofness or struggle. Communication was reserved for one's in-group, and *political* commitment to this group was only a part of one's total commitment to it. Moreover, decision making within the group and between it and other groups was based upon consensus, not majoritarianism.

To bridge these differences, or to find some method of harmonizing them, has been a formidable challenge. The same issues have existed in the ideological realm. What are the central goals of Western liberalism? Are they not to emphasize the innate dignity of the individual and give priority to his total development as the supreme *raison d'être* of the state, to give equal importance to minority rights and majority rule, to stress meaningful political competition as an essential element in freedom? But all of these goals had to confront the immediate needs and nature of Japanese society: a society lacking individualism, schooled in consensus, bred to unity, and facing the great problems of backwardness and foreign pressures. Under the circumstances, nationalism was a supremely logical force to cultivate in order to induce public sacrifice and stimulate rapid change. And tutelage of the masses by a small, cohesive elite seemed almost a compelling necessity.

It is not surprising that Meiji liberalism thus had a strongly nationalist flavor, one not wholly compatible with the current Western liberal creed. Nor is it astonishing that the later, more mature liberalism of the Taishō-Shōwa eras often sought to honor freedom and the individual by flying socialist banners, democratic and otherwise. The political ideology of modern Japan has been derived largely from the West, and the struggle to make it consistent and compatible with Japanese society has not yet been successfully resolved.

Perhaps the evolution of the Japanese parties during the period prior to 1945 can be divided into three basic eras. In the initial stage, the parties may be considered a part of the protest movement, an element in the opposition to the new Meiji government and many of its trends. This was an elitist protest. Almost

The Background

all of the participants in the party movement came from the ex-samurai class; they had been members of the feudal aristocracy. In considerable measure, it was also a sectional protest. The first parties were composed of the men from Tosa and Hizen, two ex-fiefdoms that had helped to promote the restoration of 1867 and whose representatives had subsequently participated in the new government, but who had found the supremacy of the men from Chōshū and Satsuma unpalatable. In other times, the struggle for political power would have been decided on the battlefield, and, indeed, violence did occur, culminating in the Satsuma rebellion of 1877. But dissidents now had new weapons—the words of Mill and Rousseau, the theories of liberty and constitutionalism.

The struggle was not wholly a sectional struggle for power, as the Satsuma rebellion itself would indicate. There were many issues implicit in the tremendous drive toward modernization that were of direct consequence to the ex-samurai class. Centralization of power was posed against the previously high degree of local autonomy. Urbanism and industrialization underwritten by government aid was a challenge to historic agrarian supremacy. The abolition of feudal class distinctions, the inauguration of private property, the institution of a conscription army, and many other socio-economic changes threatened the status and function of the former elite. For many of that elite, these were troubled, transitional times. What was more natural than that one of their diverse reactions would be the creation of an opposition party movement flying liberal banners and generally spearheaded by younger intellectuals?

Whatever the broad egalitarian trends in operation during the Meiji era, however, this was scarcely the era of the common man. And yet, the protest movement of this period was known as the *jiyūminken* or "civil rights" movement, and the first parties were called "popular" or "people's" parties, despite the fact that their leaders were almost exclusively ex-samurai.[2] But

[2] In addition to ex-samurai, the civil rights movement attracted various agrarian elements, particularly after 1880. Some of these politically activated persons were or became members of the prefectural assemblies, first organized in 1879. They can be regarded as the nucleus for the "pure politician" group within the parties.

this was largely because they opposed the government, the men in office. It reflected the continuing chasm that lay between the governing and the governed classes, a division that transcended all others in political importance. The official—and, more specifically, the official of the national government—had an unmatched prestige and political power. Before him, all others were commoners. The merchant or the landowner bowed low in his presence, adopted the more humble language and position, and sought his benevolence. The rule was *kanson mimpi,* "officials honored, people despised."

For modern Japan, this situation had many advantages. The premium was upon national unification and modernization in the shortest possible time. The official class functioned well in achieving these goals. It was a disciplined and relatively homogeneous group in terms of values and techniques. Its creed was strongly nationalist: service to emperor and nation. Through emphasis upon loyalty to the emperor, sectional pulls were reduced, and most officials also took a position transcendent to parties. In theory, those who served the emperor served the whole nation. Thus they could not be affiliated with parties, factions, or special interest groups, all of which represented only a segment of the people. In practice, of course, the situation was different. The official class recognized their special ties and obligations to the ex-samurai group from whence they themselves had come, and especially to that element of it that was venturing into entrepreneurship. With merchants and industrialists, new and old, the system of exchanging private gifts for government benevolence was projected forward into the modern age. Corruption, as we would measure it, did exist in this relationship, but not on the colossal scale of many societies. Indeed, the relative honesty of Meiji officialdom—or should one say the relative simplicity of their living patterns and desires?—together with their industriousness, *esprit de corps,* and rising technical proficiency contributed greatly to the rapid modernization of Japan.

In the early Meiji period, the bureaucracy was recruited largely from the politically important ex-fiefdoms, notably Chōshū and Satsuma. Leaders naturally brought in their fellow clansmen, and opponents referred to the national government as a *hambatsu,* or "clan clique." Soon a civil service system modeled after the German system was initiated, and the bureaucracy became increasingly a *gakubatsu* or "university clique." In particular, Tokyo Imperial University trained the main portion of the official elite. And in this university the German influence was strong; German legalism and jurisprudence, German philosophy and sociology, became dominant in Tokyo academic circles. The modern ideology of the Japanese official class, with its combination of conservatism and liberalism Minobe-style, was deeply influenced by this fact.[3]

During this first era, when the parties were primarily instruments of protest, the overwhelming number of officials, high and low, regarded them with hostility: parties at best were premature, unsuited to Japanese society in its current stage of development; at worst, they were subversive, dedicated to overthrowing the government. In this period, when government and the popular parties were almost always at odds, and when the techniques of peaceful opposition were largely undeveloped in Japan, violence and suppression interacted at an increasing tempo. Popular parties and the elements associated with them advocated parliamentarism, but

[3] Tokyo University was founded in 1877 and reorganized as an imperial university in 1886. Initially, British and American influence on academic policies was substantial, although the university structure itself was patterned after that of European continental universities. Increasingly, German influence was felt in such areas as curriculum and subject matter. As a result, even the university liberals derived much of their stimulus from German legal concepts and political philosophy. From these came both their methodology and their theories. Professor Minobe Tatsukichi, father of the "organistic" theory of the Japanese state, is one excellent example. For a significant study of Minobe just completed, see the doctoral dissertation of Frank O. Miller, "Minobe Tatsukichi: Interpreter of Constitutionalism in Japan" (University of California, Berkeley, 1961).

By the first decade of the twentieth century, almost all important offices in prefectural government were held by Tokyo University graduates. By the second decade. "Tōdai men" occupied most of the high civil service positions in the national government. See Kurihara Teiichi, *Chihō kankai no hensen* ("Changes in the Local Bureaucracy") (Tokyo, 1930), and Tanaka Sōgorō, *Nihon kanryō seiji shi* ("A Political History of the Japanese Bureaucracy") (Tokyo, 1954).

The Background

frequently they felt compelled to go beyond legal action. Riots, demonstrations, and violence of various types were among the weapons in their arsenal. The movement from the Diet to the streets is not a new one in Japan. Nor is the tyranny of the majority. As long as they eschewed parties of their own, the government oligarchy had little alternative except to bribe or beat their way into parliamentary control. This was the necessary price to be paid for constitutionalism. And if it were hazardous to be an opponent of the government, it was also dangerous to be a government leader. Assassination was not uncommon. Because of this fact, public security acts and other forms of official suppression could be and were justified. Thus, along with parliamentarism, modern Japan has always had a political demimonde where little quarter is asked or given—where the traditional forces, supplied with certain modern weapons, operate with scant regard for the rules of the democratic game.

Yet, as we have noted, the leadership of the first "popular parties" came from men who were not only ex-samurai, but also ex-officials in the Meiji government. Itagaki Taisuke, head of the Liberal party, and Ōkuma Shigenobu, head of the Progressive party, had both served in the top oligarchy governing Meiji Japan. Thus there has always been an ex-official quotient in the Japanese party movement, and at its summit. Who else, it might be asked, was trained, experienced, and acceptable for political leadership? But from what groups did the early Diet members of the "popular parties" come, and their rank and file membership, such as it was?

In the initial period of Japanese parliamentarism, tax and other qualifications on suffrage limited the electorate to approximately 450,000 persons out of a total population of over 30,000,000. This electorate, moreover, came overwhelmingly from the agrarian landowner class; Japan was still predominately an agricultural society and land taxes were the principal means of national revenue. There can be no doubt that the earliest Diets had a strongly agrarian flavor. The major parties, particularly the Liberals (who later became the Seiyūkai), dug their roots into rural Japan and established their connections with the prominent families whose socioeconomic position dominated this political landscape. The seemingly impregnable center of strength for the Japanese conservative parties is, and has always been, in the rural areas. But it must be remembered that rural areas were constantly becoming more complex. Many rural representatives to the Diet were engaged in mixed or essentially nonagrarian occupations. There were district entrepreneurs, professional men, and, by no means least, the "pure politicians" concerning whom we shall speak in a moment.

The popular parties also attracted a portion of the young, restless intellectuals who were stimulated by Western liberalism. The Progressive party gathered around it the Keiō University group; the Liberals had men like Nakae Chōmin and Ueki Emori. Then there were the new industrialists, a few of whom extended funds and moral support to the parties. The world of Japanese commerce and industry was still small, however, and heavily dependent upon government support. It was unwise to be found with the opposition; indeed, the business community generally shunned open political involvement of any sort, rarely running as candidates for office or serving as party sponsors. Their more usual tactic was to establish the widest possible network of personal ties with various political leaders and groups, seeking to develop a workable coalition on their behalf by exchanging private gifts for public paternalism. The commercial-industrial world of Japan has never been essentially opposed to "big government." It has merely sought to guide the power of big government toward its interests.

If one concentrates solely on the varied economic groups that were represented in the early parties, one important element is likely to be overlooked, namely the "pure politician." Some two thirds of all national Diet members attained their position after having first served in local office at the village or city level, or having been in the prefectural assembly.[4] In many cases, the only true profession of these men was politics, whatever their original occupational category. In a considerable sense, these men stood in juxtaposition to the very few ex-officials in party ranks. The pure politician was closer to Japanese grass-roots politics, closer to

[4] Cf. the chart in Oka Yoshitake (ed.), *Gendai Nihon no seiji katei* ("The Political Process in Modern Japan") (Tokyo, 1958), p. 330.

the predominant sectional and economic interests of his district, whereas the ex-official could claim a "national interest" position, an aloofness from local pressure groups and regional bias. This fact, together with their national administrative experience and continuing access to the central bureaucracy, accounts for the powerful role which the ex-officials have played as national leaders, both before and after the advent of party supremacy in Japanese politics.

If we are to summarize the first era when the Japanese parties served as part of a protest movement, we can say that the parties originally emerged as the result of a split in the ruling oligarchy and revealed the strong sectional cleavages of the early Meiji period. But they were also reflective of the impact of Western ideas and institutions upon a society in transition and when multiple pressures were operating upon the elite. The Japanese party movement in this first era was a strictly elitist movement, dominated by ex-samurai, led by frustrated members of the Meiji oligarchy. Nevertheless, it flew the banners of Western liberalism, had some appeal to commoners (in troubled agrarian regions), and voiced heterogeneous complaints: general economic dislocation; Sat-Chō political absolutism; and a "weak" foreign policy toward Korea and the West. These parties definitely vied for the nationalist symbols and, in so doing, diluted some of their vaunted liberal principles.

The emergent "popular parties" involved certain "progressive" intellectuals and a small segment of the Japanese commercial-industrial world, but the basic coloration of the parties was agrarian. Given the nature of Meiji society, this was to be expected. Despite the leadership of ex-officials, moreover, these parties contained a substantial group of "pure politicians," most of them based in the rural districts. Indeed, it was these pure politicians, with their connections reaching into the prominent social families and economic pressure groups of each district, who gave meaning to the title "popular parties," for it was this element that stood in contradistinction to the world of Japanese officialdom.

If in the first era the Japanese parties could be characterized as a part of the protest movement, in the second era the parties became sharers in political power. This was implicit in the

The Background

Meiji constitution of 1889, but movement upward for the parties was slow and uneven. They did not attain a position of quasi supremacy in Japanese politics until the end of the first World War, and they retained this position for only a little more than a decade. What were the salient characteristics of the Japanese parties in their hour of greatest triumph prior to 1945?

One of the most important trends of the second era was the progressive "bureaucratization" of the two major parties. In part, this was a necessity of constitutional politics. The Meiji constitution was heavily weighted in favor of the oligarchy and its subordinate bureaucracy, but some coöperation from the elected House of Representatives was needed, if the government was not to be stalemated. When the constitutional era opened, the gap between the government on the one hand and the "popular parties" on the other was wide. The former preached and practiced a theory of transcendentalism: "above party, on behalf of the emperor, for the nation." The latter sought to uphold varied group interests and maintain a role in decision making.

The elected House of Representatives had no legal control over the premier and his cabinet, but it had the negative power of refusing to support legislation. Japanese prewar constitutionalism in reality demanded a kind of organic unity among parties, civil bureaucracy, and military, all of which had to coöperate closely if government were to function properly, because of the distribution of powers set forth in the Meiji constitution. Thus the gap between oligarchy and parties led to troubled times. Diets were repeatedly dissolved. Bribery and intensive pressures were employed; elections were manipulated. But all of these techniques could carry a government only a certain distance. For men who would lead the nation there was ultimately no recourse except to join—and head—parties. Only then could they face the electorate with any hope.

Consequently, top members of the oligarchy abandoned transcendentalism and began to play an active role in both major parties. Itō Hirobumi inaugurated this trend by accepting the presidency of the Seiyūkai in 1900. A little over a decade later, even Katsura Tarō, protégé of General Yamagata and spokesman for the military clique, was drawn into party formation. The leading officials of the nation had found party support indispensable to their power, and leadership of the conservative parties a convenient method of effective political control. Naturally, these new leaders brought their subordinates into party activities. Thereby, a large number of top officials became party members, or, at least, became informally connected with the parties, especially those who aspired to cabinet posts. The ex-official quotient in both major parties rose, and some intraparty conflicts could be traced to the differences between the ex-official and pure politician elements. To be sure, the national bureaucracy in general stayed aloof from and hostile to the party movement, but aspirants for key political offices—the premiership and cabinet posts—were forced to join up, and this development profoundly influenced the composition of the major parties.[5]

[5] In many respects, the Japanese parties acquired their modern shape and organization during the early Taishō period. Of central importance was the interaction within the two major conservative parties between ex-official and pure politician elements. The top leaders were generally ex-officials, men like Hara Takashi and Katō Takaaki. Increasing numbers of high government officials then associated themselves with the parties in the course of seeking or attaining cabinet positions. Some became party members, especially those who were elected to the House of Representatives. Others did not become formal party members, but were labeled "Seiyū-affiliated" or "Kensei-affiliated." In addition to a larger ex-official quotient in terms of national leaders, the parties also depended heavily upon the district bureaucracy: prefectural governors—who were appointed by the interior minister from the professional administrative class—had as one of their major tasks the expansion of party strength in their area.

Local politicians coöperated with these various levels of bureaucratic leadership in order to obtain governmental benevolences for their constituencies, to strengthen their own political bases, and to beat off rivals. In this fashion, the parties established their local connections; their bases of power lay with various district bosses, who in turn had clubs or other organizations under their control. Basically, this did not represent a grass-roots party organization. Rather, it may be said that the Japanese party depended more upon an *administrative organization* —the interaction between national and prefectural administrative officials and local or Diet politicians—as the basis for party strength and

The Background

The parties were affected by other trends in Japanese society, particularly the rising importance of urban business and industry. By the close of World War I, Japan had become predominately an industrial society in terms of production; the agrarian portion remained substantial, but now the thrust period of industrialization had been reached. Japanese industry was shaped in pyramidal fashion, a mass of small and medium concerns at the base and a few large zaibatsu or so-called "financial cliques" at the top. From zaibatsu like Mitsubishi and Mitsui now came funds and even personnel for the conservative parties. In the public mind, parties and the zaibatsu were closely associated, especially after 1918, with the beginning of quasi supremacy of parties in Japanese politics.

In relative terms, agriculture declined as a political pressure group during this period, just as it declined in its percentage of the gross national product. Even after World War I, however, groups desirous of power could not ignore agriculture. In numerical terms alone, the agrarian vote was of transcendent importance, although this vote was affected by issues to a very limited extent. Still, an organization like the Imperial Agricultural Association remained a significant political force. The Seiyūkai was often called the "landowners' party" because of its extensive strength in the rural districts, and this strength was undoubtedly responsible for the fact that it was the dominant prewar party, if one considers the period as a whole. The second conservative

---

political power. Thus the parties were not—and did not need to be— mass-based organizations; they operated via the bureaucracy, in some degree as an extension of it. The early Taishō era witnessed the rising power of the parties in national politics on the one hand, and their increasing bureaucratization on the other. It is also possible, of course, to assert that along with this process of bureaucratization went the exposure of ex-officials to parliamentary politics, and that this exposure, together with the broader evolution of Japanese society and the world about it, created certain "quasi-democratic" party leaders. Men like Hara and Katō Takaaki were of a very different mold from Yamagata, or even Katsura. They symbolized "Taishō democracy" in its conservative forms. They must not be equated, however, with either the classical or "progressive" liberals typical of the Western democratic states of this period.

The Background

party, which went under a variety of names during the period 1890–1940, but is usually remembered by its last name, Minseitō, was more dependent upon urban bases of support.[6] In fact, however, both parties solicited rural support and both had important urban industrial ties. The Seiyūkai, for example, counted the giant industrial firms of Mitsui, Sumitomo, and Yasuda as supporters, while the Minseitō had the support of Mitsubishi. It is also important, however, to note that the largest percentage of votes for independent, nonparty candidates came from urban districts, indicating the relatively weaker position of the established parties among the more sophisticated elements of the Japanese electorate.

This was an era dominated by conservatism. If we waive the question of intraparty factions for the moment, the party movement of this period revolved essentially around two conservative parties whose positions on domestic and foreign policy did not differ radically. The Japanese socialist parties, after various false starts, finally emerged in 1925–26. From the beginning, the socialist movement was segmented. Three separate parties rapidly

[6] Note the following tabulation (from Shinobu, *Taishō demokurashi shi,* "A History of Taishō Democracy," III, 913):

THE URBAN-RURAL DIFFERENCE IN PARTY VOTES

	1920 Elections		1924 Elections	
	Urban (%)	Rural (%)	Urban (%)	Rural (%)
Seiyūkai	14.8	85.2	7.0	93.0
Seiyūhontō (split from Seiyūkai)	...	...	7.7	92.3
Kenseikai (later, the Minseitō)	33.3	66.7	16.7	83.3
Kakushin Club (Reform group)[a]	55.6	44.4	25.8	74.2
Jitsugyō Dōshikai[b]	...	...	76.3	23.7

[a] The Kakushin Club was formed in September, 1922, after the dissolution of the old Kokumintō. A minor party, its program was the most liberal—in Western terms—among the parties of this era.

[b] The Jitsugyō Dōshikai ("Business Fellow-Thinkers Association") was founded by Mutō Sanji as a party for progressive-minded commercial-industrial elements. Its program emphasized the separation of business from government and represented a form of liberalism, more akin to Western laissez-faire doctrines. It, too, remained a negligible political force and soon disappeared.

The Background

developed, with a fourth (the Communist party) existing underground. Although ostensibly these parties were to represent the Japanese working class, less than seven per cent of the Japanese industrial laborers were organized; labor was neither an informed nor a formidable pressure group. The socialist parties, therefore, were headed and, indeed, sustained to a considerable extent by intellectuals and a few other "middle-class" elements. Socialist party divisions were the result of complex personal and ideological cleavages. Often controversies took place at a level of theoretical abstraction that had little direct relation to the political realities of the Japanese world. The adherents of Marx, Kautsky, Bernstein, Lenin, and the Fabians joined battle, but the participants, and the audience, were few. The combined vote of the so-called proletarian parties was negligible prior to 1945. Even in the 1937 elections, after some unification had been achieved and the Social Mass party had made heavy gains, the socialist vote was less than 15 per cent of the total.

It might be argued that the prewar two-party system was essentially an artificiality, sustained by the strong feudalistic flavor that still permeated modern Japan, especially in the rural areas, and by the stunted development of organized labor. And the 1937 elections could be used to support the thesis that greater political differentiation would accompany the further development and maturation of Japanese society. There was nothing inevitable about the evolution of Japanese parliamentarism, however, as subsequent events were to prove. Democracy was first to be suppressed in Japan before being given another chance in the aftermath of defeat and revolution.

In this second era, the Japanese parties rose to a position of quasi supremacy, and, for a short time, a system of more or less automatic party governments was in existence. But neither the civil nor the military bureaucracy was basically subdued. No fundamental changes were made in the Japanese institutional structure. Some modifications were, however, made in the parties themselves, and in the party system, as prewar Japanese democracy reached its zenith point. The parties had shifted from being sectional organizations reflecting the power struggles and rivalries

The Background

within an ex-samurai class faced with multiple transitional problems, and were becoming national organizations with a more heterogeneous membership. Two pressure axes could be discerned within the dominant conservative parties: the ex-official versus the "pure politician," with the former having grown strong after the early years of struggle between officials and parties; and the agrarian versus the urban commercial-industrial interests, with the latter steadily increasing in political power and influence. Within these two axes, moreover, an element of coöperation as well as an element of conflict existed.

Prewar Japan had a two-party system, albeit one that shared power with other forces and contained many internal cleavages that altered its very nature. Thus Ozaki Yukio could assert, "We have factions in Japan, but no parties." The primary unit of Japanese politics, as of Japanese society, was the leader-follower group—the *ha,* or faction. The *ha* is derivative from the basic character of Japanese social relationships. Whether the modern faction is called a "feudal remnant" or given some other designation, it must be accorded major importance. Let us first seek to define the leader in this unit. The ideal Japanese leader is one possessing seniority, the personality and skill required to bring divergent elements together, and access to funds. He should be a man capable in effecting compromises, achieving a consensus—in these respects, a man adept at political tactics and strategy.[7] Connections in the Japanese worlds of politics and business, or, if the leader be a socialist, in the worlds of labor and the intelligentsia, are essential. There is, finally, the quality of "sincerity" and, in a broader sense, of character. The Japanese ideal in these respects cannot be easily defined. It encompasses loyalty and steadfastness

[7] In themselves, these qualities are not basically different from those sought in British or American leadership. As societies move toward modernity and mass orientation, the broad requirements of leadership take on an increasingly similar pattern and permit approximately the same range of choices. Cultural differences, however, to this point have continued to provide vital distinctions both in certain specific qualities and in general behavior patterns. We shall note this in the remarks that follow.

to one's friends and followers, courage, depth, and the possession of convictions.

Not all Japanese leaders, however, come from a single mold. Some "leaders" are chosen for their weakness, not their strength. Their tendency to be bland or neutral enables them to serve as mediators or caretakers while stronger men around them counterbalance each other without being unduly threatened by a central figure. Japanese history is replete with leaders of this type, and they exist today. Titular leadership is not necessarily to be equated with power in Japan. But there is also the strong type of leader who does in fact dominate the scene because of personal qualities such as those mentioned in the paragraph above. Many of these are "bosses" in somewhat the traditional American Tammany Hall sense, although they do not display oratorical talents or manifest publicly a colorful, extroverted personality in the manner of a James Curley or "Big Bill" Thompson—in Japan, such qualities would not be political assets. The strong, silent man whose finesse is discerned in the results that flow from actions taken in private is much closer to the Japanese ideal.

Toward his followers, the leader has the primary responsibility to provide positions, funds, and the other necessities of a good life. This union represents a political enterprise for the mutual benefit of those concerned. The stakes are high party, Diet, or administrative positions, and ample funds for election and gracious living. The more positions and money a leader can control, the more followers he is likely to draw into his camp. And, the more followers he has attracted, the more pressure he can put upon the government, his party, and private interest groups for favors and contributions.

The most important aspect of this picture, however, is that factional interest tends to take precedence over party interest and, one is tempted to say, over the public interest as well. In this special sense, can we talk meaningfully of a Japanese two-party system? To this point we must give more detailed attention later. In any case, the factional make-up of the parties also tends to make them closed organizations, exclusive clubs rather than mass membership associations. In prewar Japan, at least, the average citizen did not dream of identifying himself with a party directly. His political affiliation, if any, was with a local boss.

Hence it was not difficult to abandon party government in Japan after 1931. The third prewar era represented such abandonment and culminated in the "voluntary" dissolution of the old parties in 1940. The rise of the Japanese military was made easier by the fact that a vital link had never been established between parties and citizenry, between Diet and people. No sense of affiliation existed and, beyond that, no sense of representation, of response to "public" need and opinion. Party was rather the symbol for corruption, private interest, and unseemly struggle, in most Japanese minds. The Diet was caricatured as a zoo, and it was "they" as opposed to "we."

Consequently, the prewar parties withered after the Manchurian incident, their powers and position eaten away by nonparliamentary forces using extraparliamentary means. From the Diet to the streets—and in this era the streets were filled with the forces of the so-called Right. But the "Right" was an heterogeneous group, ranging from rebellious young officers whose socioeconomic philosophy was radical, however much they clung to the emperor and Japanese nationalism, to those ultraconservatives who saw modified Confucianism, Japanese-style, as the answer to modern problems. To these latter individuals, the Imperial Rule Assistance Association, established in 1940 to replace the parties as an advisory organization to the emperor, represented the true fulfillment of the intent of the Meiji constitution drafters.

The militarist era did not obliterate the old institutions and practices. The Meiji constitution remained unchanged. The Diet continued to operate, albeit in subdued fashion. The Imperial Rule Assistance Association was faction-ridden in the manner of all Japanese organizations, and proved to be less dynamic than had been hoped. This third era brought new elements to power, created new cliques of importance, especially within military circles, but it did not see the establishment of a mass movement, and there was no *Führer*. In the final analysis, Japanese social organization continued to triumph over the modern Western-style, individual-led,

The Background

mass-oriented movement in all its forms. But it must be recorded that the ideological content—as opposed to the organization—of Western fascism now largely replaced that of the older liberalism. There were few to mourn the passing of the parties. Little imagery of effective democracy had been established. The average citizen was not pained by the transition to militarism. Indeed, in their final years, the parties themselves had made that transition without too great a strain. Thus the stimulus for the rebuilding of Japanese democracy had to come largely from external sources. The old images and symbols derived from Japanese experience were not effective.

II

GENERAL TRENDS
IN POSTWAR
JAPANESE POLITICS

Contemporary Japan and its political trends must be viewed against the background sketched above. First, however, let us seek to classify and describe the major eras into which postwar Japanese politics should be divided.[1] Perhaps these politics, in

[1] General works dealing with postwar Japanese politics in English that should be consulted include Richard K. Beardsley, John W. Hall, and Robert E. Ward, *Village Japan* (Chicago, 1960); Hugh Borton, *Japan's Modern Century* (New York, 1955); Ardath W. Burk's forthcoming book, *Government in Japan* (New York, 1961); Nobutaka Ike, *Japanese Politics: An Introductory Survey* (New York, 1957), and his section, "Japan," in George Kahin (ed.), *Major Governments of Asia* (Ithaca, N. Y., 1958); Kazuo Kawai, *Japan's American Interlude* (Chicago, 1960); Harold Quigley and John Turner, *The New Japan: Government and Politics* (Minneapolis, 1956); Edwin O. Reischauer, *The United States and Japan* (rev. ed.; Cambridge, Mass., 1957); Herschel Webb, *An Introduction to Japan* (New York, 1955); and Chitoshi Yanaga, *Japanese People and Politics* (New York, 1956).

broadest terms, can be divided into two eras, although many re-
finements and subdivisions are necessary. The first era was that
of upheaval, change, and fluidity. It encompassed the period of
American occupation from September, 1945, to January, 1949.
Viewed from any standpoint, this was a tumultuous era. In terms
of American policy, it was the period of punishment and reform.
In terms of Japanese attitudes, it was a period of reaction against
old leaders and old traditions, a reaction against the past, and
hence of receptivity to change. It was also a period when American
governors took the initiative, with the aid of some classically
"minority" forces within Japanese society. The old forces that had
been dominant in Japan, now largely passive, were in many cases
forced onto the defensive and into retreat.

The final months of this first period, however, represented a transitional phase. American emphasis upon punishment
and reform changed to a policy stressing the rehabilitation and
reconstruction of the Japanese economy. American policies and
attitudes, influenced partly by international considerations, became
increasingly conservative. Japanese attitudes also began to change.
The combination of intensive self-criticism and passivity began to
fade away, replaced by a more complex psychology. Gradually, a
reaction to the Occupation itself developed. Its errors of omission
and commission, its excesses and obvious absurdities, came into
focus. Once again, some retreat from a high tide of Westernism

---

For general works in Japanese see Inoki Masamichi (ed.), *Nihon
no nidai seitō* ("The Two Parties of Japan") (Tokyo, 1956); Oka
(ed.), *op. cit.; Sengo Nihon no kokka kenryoku* ("Political Power in
Postwar Japan"), edited by the Contemporary History Study Group
(Tokyo, 1960); Shinobu Seisaburō *et al.* (eds.), *Saisei to hatten*
("Rebirth and Development"), Vol. III of *Gendai hantaisei undō shi*
("History of Contemporary Opposition Political Movements") (Tokyo,
1960); Soma Masao, *Sengo seiji shi* ("History of Postwar Politics")
(2 vols.; Tokyo, 1959); *Taishū undō to seiji katei* ("Mass Movements
and the Political Process"), Vol. IV of *Gendai Nihon no seiji to keizai*
("Politics and Economics of Modern Japan") (Tokyo, 1959); "Tennō
Sei" ("The Emperor System"), a special issue of *Shisō* ("Thought"),
June, 1952; Togawa Isamu, *Shōwa gendai shi* ("Modern History of
Shōwa") (Tokyo, 1959); and Yanaibara Tadao (ed.), *Sengo Nihon
shōshi* ("Short History of Postwar Japan") (2 vols.; Tokyo, 1957).

commenced in certain areas. Or was this merely an attempt to pay homage to the realities of Japanese society, as the conservatives insisted? Since the early Meiji era, there had been a certain swing of the pendulum; eras of extensive Western borrowing had been followed by periods of absorption and even retrenchment, although the retreat had never been uniform, nor was it now.

Passiveness, moreover, declined. The *Japanese* quotient in Japanese politics inevitably increased, and the authority of the Occupation, which had once been omnipresent, began to recede. To be sure, the Occupation had never really understood or controlled the inner recesses of Japanese politics. But for a time its operations were extensive enough to render the "opposition"— indeed, all indigenous forces—largely dependent and subordinate in connection with basic policy decisions. There was the curious and oft-noted spectacle of a military government superimposed upon a constitutional government and attempting to persuade and coerce, to tutor a nation in democracy. Perhaps the paradox involved here was no greater than that involved in any system of tutelage which has democratic goals.

In any case, toward the end of this first period, the rise of Japanese nationalism as a reaction to the Occupation in all its aspects had begun, and the quotient of Japanese authority in the political scene had started to increase.[2] Before suggesting the

[2] Any division of postwar Japanese politics is arbitrary in some measure, and one may certainly argue with the demarkations suggested here. We might suggest a second and slightly different approach, one which places somewhat more emphasis upon indigenous factors and somewhat less upon American policy changes:

One may consider the period down to 1949 as a reaction to defeat in war, a period marked by great fluidity and instability in Japanese politics. This period ended with the Yoshida cabinet which came to power in late 1948 and was overwhelmingly confirmed by the election of January, 1949. The next era represented a reaction to instability, upheaval, and, in some senses, the radical democratization program itself. With American support (United States policy had changed), the Yoshida era was characterized by conservative readjustments on the domestic scene and close relations with the United States on the international front.

By 1951, however, there were numerous indications of a rising renature of the second period, however, let us look at the first era in somewhat greater detail.

The early postwar period in Japan, down to 1949, was quasi-revolutionary. The fact that the revolution was bloodless and mainly induced by external forces is important, but it does not alter the radical character of many of the changes accomplished or initiated during this period. As is well known, the substance of the revolution was provided by the American Occupation. Radical antimilitary and "anti-Fascist" measures were accompanied by a vast array of American reform programs, partly tailored to Japanese society. This was the period when the United States turned Japan into a "Switzerland of the Far East" and, indeed, moved her beyond Switzerland by outlawing military forces and war as an instrument of Japanese foreign policy. In rapid fashion, millions of men were demobilized and the old military branches of government were abolished; the once-powerful military pressure groups (including veterans' associations) disappeared. The widespread purges which began in early 1946 contributed mightily to the appearance of new faces in Japanese politics. Professional military men, government candidates in the Tōjō-sponsored Diet elections of 1942, and all leaders of ultranationalist societies were "permanently" barred from political officeholding. Overnight, a substantial number of "pure politicians" and ex-officials from conservative ranks were banished to the shadows. From those

---

action to the Occupation. Japanese nationalism in a variety of forms was beginning to make itself felt. In domestic politics, this helped to forward intraparty resistance to Yoshida, the gradual increase of socialist strength, and the movement of the socialists to the left. All of these trends were in some measure symbols of the quest for an higher quotient of independence vis-à-vis the United States. Readjustments did take place in this relationship. Between 1955 and 1958, with the establishment—at least temporarily—of a "two-party system," Japanese politics seemed to have reached a plateau, a new degree of stability, with the relative positions of the major political forces in the country essentially fixed. Political instability in Japan surely existed, but it was a more subtle force, not easily detected merely by looking at election returns or reading other surface indications. This last point, of course, we shall seek to develop further as we go along.

shadows, individual leaders sometimes continued to wield political power, but their role could not be precisely the same as when they operated from an open, legal position.

As the purges sought to retire many of the old conservative elite, the reforms were aimed at raising up new forces in Japanese society or, at least, creating a more nearly equal balance of competitive pressure groups. The land reform program is familiar to all, at least in its broad outlines. Tenancy was reduced to less than 10 per cent of the total number of farm families, absentee landlordism was largely eliminated, and a considerable equity in landownership was introduced. While this program was not executed without some evasions, violations, and injustices of various sorts, it was certainly one of the most thorough land reform programs ever carried out by a non-Communist society. Economic distinctions among Japanese agrarian families were greatly reduced, although social distinctions, a legacy of the past, continued. The quest for an independent yeomanry might have been imperfectly realized, but the land reform program certainly left its mark on Japanese agrarian society, especially when coupled with educational and other sociopolitical changes.[3]

Meanwhile, a deconcentration program was launched against Japanese big business, the special target being the old zaibatsu. This program did not long continue, and it fell far short of its initial objectives. Nevertheless, cartels and holding companies were eliminated or reduced, at least temporarily. The base of big business was somewhat broadened, and this had the effect also of broadening business-political relations. These relations were no longer confined primarily to five or six giant firms. Larger segments of the business community were now involved, often through their national and regional organizations.[4] It was also during this

[3] In English, one should consult R. P. Dore, *Land Reform in Japan* (Berkeley and Los Angeles, 1959).

[4] For an English-language study of Occupation deconcentration attempts see T. A. Bisson, *Zaibatsu Dissolution in Japan* (Berkeley and Los Angeles, 1954).

For postwar business-political relations, see the following Japanese articles and books: Hayashi Shōzō, "The Power Elite in Japan," *Chūō Kōron* ("Central Review"), January, 1960, pp. 146–157; Katō Shimei,

period that the labor movement was given great impetus by Occupation support. Organized labor finally became more than a negligible force in Japanese society and politics. If it was no longer negligible, however, it still occupied a distinctly minority status, and it remained divided internally and faced with multiple problems.[5]

"The Real Character of the Political League of Small and Medium Enterprises," *ibid.,* May, 1958, pp. 102–108; Keizai Dantai Rengōkai ("Federation of Economic Associations"), *Keidanren no jūnen* ("Ten Years of The Federation of Economic Associations") (Tokyo, 1956); Keizai Dōyūkai ("Economic Friends' Association"), *Keizai Dōyūkai jūnen shi* ("A Ten-Year History of the Economic Friends' Association") (Tokyo, 1956); Kobayashi Naoki, "The Process of Legislating the Minor Enterprise Organization Law," *Shakai kagaku kiyo* ("Social Science Bulletin") (Tokyo, 1957), pp. 1–104; Nihon Keieisha Dantai Remmei ("Japan Federation of Employers' Associations"), *Jūnen no ayumi* ("Ten Years of Progress") (Tokyo, 1958); Sakamoto Fujiyoshi, "Employers in Japan," *Chūō Kōron,* October, 1960, pp. 142–156; and the Economics Section of the *Yomiuri Shimbun, Shin zaibatsu monogatari* ("Stories of the New Zaibatsu") (Tokyo, 1956).

[5] For English-language works on the postwar Japanese labor movement see James C. Abegglen, *The Japanese Factory: Aspects of Its Social Organization* (Glencoe, Ill., 1958); Solomon B. Levine, *Industrial Relations in Postwar Japan* (Urbana, Ill., 1958); and Robert A. Scalapino, "Japan," in Walter Galenson (ed.), *Labor and Economic Development* (New York, 1959).

In Japanese, see Fujita Wakao, *Dai ni kumiai* ("The Second Union") (Tokyo, 1955); Hidaka Rokurō *et al.,* "Trade Unions and Political Consciousness," *Shisō,* July, 1955, pp. 37–56; Hosoya Matsuta, *Nihon no rōdō kumiai undō* ("The Labor Union Movement in Japan") (Tokyo, 1958); Kitagawa Ryūkichi *et al.,* "Sōhyō and Zenrō," *Chūō Kōron,* April, 1900, pp. 103–125; Matsushita Keiichi, "The Political Activities of the Trade Unions," in *Nempō seijigaku* ("Political Science Yearbook") (Tokyo, 1960), pp. 86–112; Ōkochi Kazuo, *Sengo Nihon no rōdō undō* ("The Labor Movement in Postwar Japan") (Tokyo, 1955); Ōkochi Kazuo *et al.* (eds.), *Rōdō kumiai no kōzō to kinō* ("Structure and Functions of Labor Unions") (Tokyo, 1959); *Rōdō undō shiryō* ("Materials on the Labor Movement"), a yearly publication of the Ministry of Labor (Rōdō Shō); Saitō Ichirō, *Sōhyō shi* ("History of Sōhyō") (Tokyo, 1957); *Sengo Nihon rōdō undō shi* ("History of the Postwar Japanese Labor Movement") (2 vols., Tokyo, 1956); Shakai Kagaku Kenkyūjo ("Institute of Social

Occupational reforms also involved sweeping institutional changes. The constitution of 1947 was one of the great monuments to this era. This constitution provided a new framework for Japanese democracy, one that placed the Diet, and hence the parties, in the center of the political stage. Swept away was the fiction of imperial absolutism, and the menace of a system that placed a premium upon the organic unity of parties, civil officials, and the military. The new system was a reflection of Anglo-American experience. That much of it was foreign to Japanese experience could not be denied. The unanswered question was whether the whole network of social changes would bring Japanese society into conformity with the new political structure, or, at least, give society and institutions a chance to evolve toward each other.

These were the most basic developments of the first period that affected Japanese politics. What were the salient characteristics of those politics, with special reference to leadership and the parties? We may note first the emergence of a multiparty system, far more complex than the system that existed in prewar Japan. Five significant national parties took shape, together with a huge number of provincial or local parties. At the national level, the two prewar conservative parties were quickly reëstablished under changed names and somewhat altered membership. Hatoyama Ichirō, a veteran Seiyūkai leader, took charge of the organization of the Liberal party, which was officially inaugurated on November 9, 1945. In the same period, prewar Minseitō leaders, particularly the Machida faction, uniting with the old Nakajima faction of the Seiyūkai, formed the Progressive party. Machida Chūji was elected head in mid-December, and until the political purges of early 1946 the Progressive membership roster included the overwhelming majority of the wartime Diet members.[6]

Sciences," Tokyo University), *Sengo rōdō kumiai no jittai* ("The Actual Conditions of the Postwar Labor Unions") (Tokyo, 1950); Takano Minoru, *Nihon no rōdō undō* ("The Japanese Labor Movement") (Tokyo, 1958); Tanabashi Yasusuke, *Sengo rōdō undō shi* ("History of the Postwar Labor Movement") (Tokyo, 1959); and Yamazaki Gorō, *Nihon rōdō undō shi* ("History of the Japanese Labor Movement") Tokyo, 1957).

[6] For a summary of postwar party developments in English see

With considerable effort, the Japanese socialists launched a unified Social Democratic party in early November of 1945. All of the divergent factions that had generally been split into separate parties in the prewar era agreed to work together, but the basis for both ideological and personal unity was precarious.[7] On October 4, the first legal Japanese Communist party

Robert A. Scalapino, "Japan: Between Traditionalism and Democracy," in Sigmund Neumann (ed.), *Modern Political Parties* (Chicago, 1956).

In Japanese, for a variety of views on the conservative parties, see Adachi Kōichi *et al.,* "We Are the Local Organizers of the Liberal Democratic Party," *Chūō Kōron,* April, 1960, pp. 88–102; Fujiwara Hirotatsu, *Hoshu dokusai ron* ("On Conservative Dictatorship") (Tokyo, 1957), and "The Political Sense of the Liberal Democratic Party," *Chūō Kōron,* February, 1959, pp. 58–84; Itagaki Shinsuke, *Kono jiyūtō* ("This Liberal Party") (2 vols., Tokyo, 1956); and Watanabe Tsuneo, *Habatsu* ("The Cliques") (Tokyo, 1958).

There are also some useful memoirs and biographies of postwar conservative leaders: Fujiyama Aiichi, *Watakushi no jijoden* ("My Autobiography") (Tokyo, 1958); Hatoyama Ichirō, *Watakushi no jijoden* (Tokyo, 1951), and *Aru daigishi no seikatsu to iken* ("The Life and Thoughts of a Certain Diet Representative") (Tokyo, 1952); Kōno Ichirō, *Ima dakara hanasō* ("Now I Can Speak") (Tokyo, 1957); the Miki Club (ed.), *Miki Bukichi* (Tokyo, 1958); Mitarai Tatsuo, *Miki Bukichi* (Tokyo, 1958); Shigemori Kyūji, *Miki Bukichi taikōki* ("The Heroic Record of Miki Bukichi") (Tokyo, 1956); Ōno Bamboku, *Bamboku hōdan* ("Bamboku's Wild Talk") (Tokyo, 1955); the Shidehara Club (ed.), *Shidehara Kijūrō* (Tokyo, 1955); Takamiya Tahei, *Ningen Ogata Taketora* ("Ogata Taketora as a Man") (Tokyo, 1958); Yoshida Shigeru, *Kaiko jūnen* ("Ten Years' Reminiscences") (4 vols., Tokyo, 1957–58).

[7] For Japanese works on the postwar socialist party see Hirose Kenichi, *Saha Shakaitō no jittai* ("The Actual Condition of the Left-Wing Socialist Party") (Tokyo, 1955); Hisayoshi Takeo, "The Organizational Power of the Progressive Parties," *Shisō,* June, 1959, pp. 82–90; Kōno Mitsu, *Nihon shakaiseitō shi* ("History of the Japanese Socialist Parties") (Tokyo, 1960); Masujima Hiroshi, "How the Socialist Party Should Escape Stagnation," *Chūō Kōron,* October, 1959, pp. 62–73; Masujima Hiroshi *et al.,* "The Meaning of the Socialist Split," *Sekai* ("World"), December, 1959, pp. 50–66; Anonymous, "Japan Current: The Socialist Party in Agony," *ibid.,* November, 1959, pp. 254–259; Matsushita Keiichi, "The Two Hearts of Democratic Socialism," *Chūō Kōron,* December, 1959, pp. 73–83; Nakatsu

was organized by Tokuda Kyūichi and some other veteran Communists, many of whom had just been released after nearly two decades in prison.[8] Finally, the Coöperative party was a fifth national party of some importance to make its appearance in late 1945, organized by a small group of Diet members with rural and middle-class interests, and dedicated to the coöperative movement.

These five parties represented as wide an ideological spectrum as could be found in any modern state. To be sure, Japanese conservatism in this period was not certain what it could or should conserve. Relatively strange terms, such as "individual freedom," "human liberties," and "free enterprise," crept into the conservative vocabulary. Gone was the old emphasis upon *kokutai*, unswerving loyalty to the emperor, the importance of sublimating the individual to the group, the superiority of Japanism, and the messianic mission of Japan in Asia. Yet the conservatives, particu-

Kenji, *Shin sayoku ron* ("Discourse on the New Left") (Kyoto, 1960); Shimazaki Yuzuru, "For the Advance of the Japanese Socialist Party," *Chūō Kōron*, February, 1959, pp. 32–44; Sone Eki *et al.,* "Questions to the Socialist Party," *ibid.,* March, 1960, pp. 97–113; Taguchi Fukuji, "A Discourse on the Japanese Socialist Party," *ibid.,* September, 1958, pp. 124–143, "The Left Wing in Japan," *ibid.,* April, 1960, pp. 146–157, "Changes in the Political Situation and the Japanese Socialist Party," *ibid.,* September, 1960, pp. 80–91, and "A Discourse on the Japanese Socialist Party," *ibid.,* February, 1961, pp. 26–49; Yanada Koki, *Nihon Shakaitō* ("The Japanese Socialist Party") (Tokyo, 1956); Yamazaki Hiroshi, *Nihon Shakaitō jūnen shi* ("A Ten-Year History of the Japanese Socialist Party") (Tokyo, 1956).

For interesting autobiographies see Nishio Suehiro, *Taishū to tomo ni* ("With the People") (Tokyo, 1951); Suzuki Mosaburō, *Aru shakaishugisha no hansei* ("Half the Life of a Certain Socialist") (Tokyo, 1958), and *Watakushi no ayunda michi* ("The Road I Walked") (Tokyo, 1960).

[8] For some Japanese works on the Communist party see Koyama Hirotake, *Sengo Nihon Kyōsantō shi* ("History of the Postwar Japanese Communist Party") (Tokyo, 1958); Murakami Kanji, *Nihon Kyōsantō* ("The Japanese Communist Party") (Tokyo, 1956); Nikkan Rōdō Tsūshinsha (ed.), *Sengo Nihon kyōsanshugi undō shi* ("History of the Communist Movement in Postwar Japan") (Tokyo, 1955), Ōi Hirosuke, *Sayoku Tennōsei* ("The Left Wing Emperor System") (Tokyo, 1956); Tagawa Kazuo, *Nihon Kyōsantō shi* ("History of the Japanese Communist Party") (Tokyo, 1960).

larly the Liberals, fought a stubborn rear-guard action to defend some of the traditional values which they held dear, such as the emperor system and a modified Confucian ethic. Western values had to be synthesized with these classical values in the true conservative mind. The Progressives thought more in social welfare terms. Their goal was a reformed capitalism, with safeguards and benefits for previously dispossessed groups. In them, incidentally, many Americans saw a possible "third force" standing between the unreconstructed right and the socialists. The socialists themselves ranged over a vast doctrinal field from Fabianism to Marxism. The Communists, of course, took their position with Marx-Leninism as interpreted by Moscow. Never in their history had the Japanese people had such a complete doctrinal choice, although to put the point in this fashion may be misleading, for in reality the Japanese electorate was not highly conscious of doctrine, and voting behavior was based much more heavily upon other considerations. Nevertheless, the choice was present, and, at least, more real than in the prewar period.

In addition to the five national parties that had emerged by the end of 1945, there was a staggering number of local or prefectural parties. Some of these were no more than one-man, one-party organizations, parties on paper but not in fact. But at the time of the first postwar general election, in April, 1946, about 350 local parties existed. Typical examples were the Hyūga (Miyazaki Prefecture) Democratic party, the Miyagi (Prefecture) Local party, and the Hokkaidō Political Union. The number of independents running for office without any party label was also large. To some extent, this reflected Japanese tradition. The independent had always played a significant role in Japanese politics, although the number of independents had declined during the prewar era of party supremacy.[9]

[9] In the early postwar elections, to be sure, it is important to distinguish among various types of minor parties and independent candidates. Some were really "fronts" for the national parties which were still in the process of formation. Many, as we shall soon note, represented the natural political expression of Japanese social organization at the local or regional level at a time when national authority and coördination were weak. It is also true that running for public office

Trends in Postwar Japanese Politics

These initial trends testified to the chaotic condition of postwar Japanese politics in the first years after military defeat. To be sure, one must not ignore the large measure of continuity in the political scene. All of the national parties, for example, had previously existed in some form, with the exception of the Coöperative party, which soon disappeared. The initial leadership and programs of these parties, moreover, were strongly suggestive of the past despite the innovations noted above. Indeed, the factor of continuity in Japanese politics from the prewar period down to the present seems very large in retrospect. Contemporary Japan is a curious mixture wherein old political forms and forces have shown a remarkable capacity to survive—thus far—in the midst of rapid socioeconomic change. Yet in the immediate postwar period it was not clear that these forms and forces would survive. At the height of the purge, in the period beginning with early 1946, Japanese politics was in turmoil. Most of the famous conservative politicians had been removed from open leadership. The Occupation was riding roughshod over those who remained. Old institutions had been scrapped. The interest groups previously dominant had been put under intensive pressure. The indigenous forces at the national level were weak, limited in their powers, and—especially the conservatives—uncertain of their future.

Under the circumstances, perhaps it was natural that local parties should develop in many areas. National politics was chaotic, and even the normal channels of communication were confused. But in this critical period there remained the small leader-follower group, that indestructable unit of Japanese politics. Generally, this group had a provincial base. The nature of Japanese organization acted in some measure to sustain provincialism despite the powerful pressures that had operated against it since the Meiji era. There were other factors that helped to buttress the tendency toward localism and independent candidates during this period.

---

had a new glamor during this early period, due in part to the extensive publicity being given "demokurashi" and the very considerable vacuum of power left by the removal or retirement of various old elements, hence the heightened opportunities. A few candidates even ran for office primarily to publicize their products or businesses, seeking to take advantage of the spotlight being thrown upon the election process.

Trends in Postwar Japanese Politics

Previously, the national parties had almost no grass-roots organization; individual Diet members, instead of being dependent upon the national party, generally had their own local organizations. Hence it was easy to operate via old or new "local" parties in a time of relaxed national power, of centrifugal tendencies.

The scattered, heterogeneous nature of Japanese politics in the early postwar period is underscored by the statistics that pertain to the election of April, 1946.[10] Three hundred and sixty-three separate "parties" participated in that election, if one counts every local organization claiming party status. Some 2,770 candidates competed for the 466 seats in the House of Representatives, an average of 5.9 candidates for each seat. Of those candidates, 52 per cent ran as members of minor parties or as independents. The election results were also interesting. Three hundred and seventy-seven of the 464 house seats, or 81 per cent, went to "new members," that is, members not previously elected. One hundred and thirty-three elected members, or 29 per cent, were from minor parties or were elected as independents. This represented nearly one third of the first postwar house.

Naturally, political upheaval and change was at its height in the 1946 election. In the election of May, 1947, the number of candidates for the lower house was 1,590, or 3.4 times the available seats (as compared with 5.9 in the 1946 election).[11] Thirty-two per cent of these candidates (505) were from minor parties or independents. Eighty per cent (1,300) were individuals not previously members of the house. In terms of the results, 48 per cent (222) of the elected candidates were new members. Fourteen per cent (67) were from minor parties or independents.

Even in the election of January, 1949, the element of

[10] In December, 1945, the election law was revised. Women were given the vote, the voting age was lowered from twenty-five to twenty, and a limited plural-ballot system was established. These rules applied in the 1946 elections.

[11] Prior to the 1947 election, the electoral system was changed. From that election to the present, each Japanese voter has had only one vote, with three to five representatives elected from each district, depending upon its size. This fact must be kept in mind when comparing the 1946 election with those that followed.

change was significant, although the indices showed a rising degree of political stability.[12] In this election there were 1,364 candidates (2.9 times the number of seats). This number included 865 individuals (63 per cent) not previously members of the house, and 269 minor party and independent candidates (19 per cent). In the new house then elected, 41 per cent (192) were new members, and 11 per cent (50) were from minor parties or independents.

These figures reveal some interesting aspects of Japanese parliamentarism between 1946 and 1949. The first postwar Diets (referring here specifically to the House of Representatives) were composed overwhelmingly of individuals newly come to national politics. And, in general, their tenure in office was brief. In short, these first Diets were characterized by a large number of novices in the national legislature, and a very high turnover. It is not surprising, of course, that over 80 per cent of the house members elected in April, 1946, were first-term members. Most of the old-time Diet members had been purged and were not allowed to run for reëlection.[13] However, nearly half of those elected to the 1947 House of Representatives were new members, and over 40 per cent of the 1949 House fell into this category.

It is possible to exaggerate the element of newness in the Japanese political scene of this period. If one examines statistics pertaining to the elections of 1947 and 1949, it will be seen that approximately 50 per cent of the elected conservative members and 40 per cent of the elected socialist members had previous experience either in national appointive office (civil service) or in prefectural or local elective office.[14] Specifically, in 1947, 14 per cent of the Liberal party house members were ex-officials, and an additional 40 per cent had previously been either prefectural assemblymen or local officeholders. In 1949 these percentages were 17 per cent and 35 per cent, respectively. The 1947 figures for the Democratic

[12] See Chart 8 (Appendix).

[13] For an excellent English-language study of the purges, see Hans H. Baerwald, *The Purge of the Japanese Leaders under the Occupation* (Berkeley and Los Angeles, 1959).

[14] See Chart 8.

(Progressive) party[15] were: ex-officials, 8 per cent; prefectural or local elective officials, 40 per cent. In 1949 the figures were 17 per cent and 39 per cent. The number of ex-officials in the socialist ranks was small (2 per cent in 1947, none in 1949), but the number of members who had previously been assemblymen or locally elected officials was surprisingly high (38 per cent in 1947, 43 per cent in 1949).

In these figures, once again one notices the relatively heavy strength of the local politicians as opposed to the former members of the national bureaucracy, to the ex-official or centralized government contingent. It should be noted, however, that the top leaders of the conservative movement during this period came from the ex-official group. In part, this was due to the extensive purges which had decimated the senior "pure politician" ranks. Thus, the most eligible conservative leaders were men like Shidehara Kijūrō, Yoshida Shigeru, and Ashida Hitoshi, men who came from the so-called "British" or "Anglo-American" clique of the Foreign Ministry and who were relatively untarnished with a militarist past. These men maintained ex-official leadership of the Japanese conservative parties in this difficult, fluid period.

Yet another modification of fairly major proportions must be made to the general theme that this first period was one of political change, fluidity, and upheaval. In one sense (if we waive the question of intraparty factionalism for the moment), Japanese party politics were perhaps not as badly fragmented as appears at first glance. We have seen that local party–independent strength declined sharply after the chaotic 1946 election. In addition, not all of the five major national parties were serious contenders for political leadership or even vital elements in a coalition. The Coöperative party polled 3.2 per cent of the vote in the 1946 election and

---

[15] This party, first named "Progressive Party" (Nihon Shimpotō) in November, 1945, shifted to the designation "Democratic Party" (Minshutō) in March, 1947, at the time of the merger with the Coöperative party. In April, 1950, it became the "People's Democratic Party" (Kokumin Minshutō), and in February, 1952, the "Reform Party" (Kaishintō). In November, 1954, it again shifted, to "Japan Democratic Party" (Nihon Minshutō).

obtained 14 Diet seats. It reached its peak in the April, 1947, election with 7 per cent of the vote and 29 seats. In the January, 1949, election it had declined to 3.4 per cent of the total vote and 14 seats. Shortly thereafter it dissolved, with the majority of its members joining the Democratic party. The Communist party polled 3.8 per cent of the vote in the 1946 election and elected five Diet members. It obtained 3.7 per cent of the vote in 1947, and four Diet seats. Its peak was reached in 1949, when it polled 9.7 per cent of the total vote and elected 35 Diet members under unusual circumstances; temporarily, the socialists were badly discredited and divided. But as we shall later note, the subsequent Cominform criticism of Nosaka Sanzō and the onset of the Korean war inaugurated an era of division, quasi-legality, and general weakness for the Communists. They have polled less than 3 per cent of the total vote since 1949.

In reality, therefore, the Japanese multiparty system of this period was built essentially around three parties, the Liberals, the Democrats (Progressives), and the Social Democrats or Socialists. Each of these parties had prewar roots, as we have seen. The Liberals had their nucleus in the old Seiyūkai. The Democrats had major ties with the old Minseitō. The Social Democratic or Socialist party represented a valiant attempt to unify the three or four prewar proletarian parties. Any basic difference from the prewar political picture seemed to hinge upon two factors: first, the strength and basic policies of the Social Democratic party; second, the nature of the postwar Progressive (Democratic) party.

The Japanese prewar party system, as we have noted, was a "two-party system" partly because socioeconomic and political conditions did not permit a unified, powerful socialist or labor party. In the last free election of the prewar period, however, the Social Mass party had scored significant gains. In this sense, the first postwar elections might be viewed primarily as a continuation of a trend already under way. But the critical question was whether the combination of war defeat and destruction, Occupation reforms, conservative confusion, and popular unrest would transform the Social Democratic party into a major party, even *the* major party.

The answer to this question, at least the short-range

answer, was disappointing to the socialists. The Social Democratic party immediately became a major party, but it fell far short of becoming the majority party. As a result, certain new problems for the socialists were added to the old ones. In the 1946 election, the socialists polled nearly 18 per cent of the vote and obtained 92 seats. The most substantial gain came in 1947, when the Social Democratic party obtained 26 per cent of the vote and 143 seats in the lower house. But this did not prove to be a political "take-off" period, as the socialists had hoped. Instead, it inaugurated an era of troubles. With less than one third of the total vote or Diet seats, the socialists came to office by organizing a coalition with the Democrats and Coöperatives. For complex reasons that involved Occupation policy, leadership problems, and policy discrepancies, this coalition was a failure.

It is ironic, perhaps, that the major Occupation reforms were engineered while Japanese conservatives held all major offices, whereas the advent of the Japanese socialists to high office was accompanied by an Occupation shift from reform to rehabilitation. Thus, as the conservatives had been forced to execute radical reforms, the socialists were forced to effect retreat, retrenchment, and austerity. Under circumstances where there were really two governments, the Occupation and the Japanese, it was extraordinarily difficult for the Japanese parties to remain true to their principles and policies or, indeed, to bear any responsibility for the execution of policy. Inevitably, this was a confusing period for leaders and people alike. And it was the socialist misfortune to come into partial power at a time when circumstances both in Japan and abroad dictated a basic shift in Occupation policy away from socialist interests. American policy, to be sure, had never been aimed at achieving socialism, but its zenith period, the era of punishment and reform, clearly gave to the Japanese socialists some advantages not present when the emphasis was shifted to economic rehabilitation.

There were other factors, however, that plagued the socialist cause. The policy and personal differences between the socialists and the Democrats proved too great to permit an effective coalition. Thus the Katayama-Ashida and Ashida-Katayama cabinets were undistinguished in performance, lacking in dynamism and initiative. Not a single piece of major socialist legislation was enacted during this period, and on several issues, such as the nationalization of the coal mines, the socialists suffered major defeats. Moreover, the fact of coalition exacerbated the deep cleavages among the socialists themselves. Popular fronts, coalitions, and alliances in domestic politics often have serious internal repercussions within some of the participant parties. In retrospect, the coalition era of 1947–48 appears to have been decidedly unfortunate for the socialists for a number of reasons, although admittedly one cannot gauge the alternatives with any certainty. At any rate, the coalition ended in failure, crowned at the end by scandal. The Social Democratic party slipped badly in the 1949 election, polling only 13.5 per cent of the vote and securing a mere 48 seats in the lower house. And the climb back up has proven slow, as we shall see.

Thus when the first period of postwar Japanese politics ended, the Social Democratic party neither held power nor appeared as a formidable contender for power. Ideologically, it was badly split, and, indeed, its right and left wings were now moving toward a complete break. The so-called right wing took its basic stand with parliamentarism and social democracy; it rejected Marxism as a philosophic base, and approached the British Fabian position in general outlook. As in philosophic attitude, so in foreign policy it tended to lean toward the West, although many of its members favored a greater degree of nonalignment and independence than the conservatives were prepared to offer. The left wing remained wedded to Marxism, often of a curiously old-fashioned, Germanic type. Their ideological position, scarcely changed in a quarter of a century, bore the clear imprint of the *Rōnō-Kōza* factional debates which had preoccupied Japanese Marxists in the late 1920's and early 1930's. The left wing was militantly neutralist, and some elements were vigorously anti-American, seemingly close to the Communists. The possibility of true reconciliation between these two general groups of socialists was remote, despite the continuous efforts that were made. Socialist unity, moreover, was made increasingly difficult because of world trends, the growing estrangement between the "Free" and "Communist" worlds.

As we have suggested, the nature of the Democratic party was also a matter of consequence to Japanese politics and the party system. Would this party be a "third force," as some hoped? There was a certain basis in fact for this hope. One wing of the Democratic party was of social reform type. Indeed, postwar Japanese politics has often echoed to the rumors of coalition or union between the "progressive conservatives" and the "moderate socialists," between the left wing of the Democrats and the right wing of the Social Democrats. Down to the present, such ideas have continued to exist.

In fact, however, the coalition of 1947–48, which was largely constructed by these groups, failed to achieve positive results. Instead, it left a legacy of bitterness and tended to split off the more radical (and conservative) elements within the two parties without truly uniting the moderates. And, in the final analysis, the Democratic party overwhelmingly cast its lot with the Liberals. Such effect as it might have upon policy was exercised here, not with the socialists. And, in fact, the Democrats, with few exceptions, were always much closer to their fellow conservatives than to the socialists of whatever persuasion.

When the first period is viewed in this light, the continuous conservative dominance of postwar Japan stands out. The conservatives, whether united or divided, have polled close to two thirds of the votes at all times. Their supremacy has been seriously challenged only once—in the 1947–48 period, when the crucial issue was the direction that the Democratic party, or a substantial segment of it, would take. That issue was resolved decisively in favor of conservatism. In the 1946 election, the Liberal party polled 24 per cent of the vote and obtained 140 lower house seats; the Progressives polled 19 per cent and got 94 seats. In addition, it must be remembered that the preponderance of minor party and independent victors were conservative. In the 1947 election, the Liberals and Democrats got 27 and 25 per cent of the vote and 131 and 121 Diet seats, respectively. In 1949, however, the Demo-

cratic-Liberal party soared to a spectacular victory, with 44 per cent
of the vote and 264 Diet seats, whereas the Democrats shared in
coalition defeat by dipping to 16 per cent of the vote and 69 seats.
The total vote of the two parties was some 60 per cent, a figure
which could be augmented by adding the minor party–independent
conservative vote.

Thus the designation of the Japanese party system of
the early postwar era as a multiparty system requires substantial
qualification. Two of the five national parties were never critical
—or even vital—factors in the national scene. They could not and
did not play the role of political balance wheels, a classic and
important role in any multiparty system. The one party that could
and did play that role briefly was the Democratic party, and the
1947–48 period was the only period when Japan has had an
operative multiparty system. By 1949 the Liberal party had become
the dominant party in Japan, and, as the Social Democratic party
moved left, the chances of coalition between it and the Democrats
became more and more remote.

Perhaps now the earlier generalizations concerning the
first general period of postwar Japanese politics can be properly
qualified and refined. We have referred to it as a period of upheaval,
change, and fluidity. This it was. As we have noted, it began with
high quotients of "newness" and diversity in national politics, and
although these declined they were still substantial as late as 1949.
Moreover, major fluctuations in Japanese voting behavior took
place during this period. Note, for example, that the Liberals went
from 24 per cent in 1946 and 27 per cent in 1947 to 44 per cent
in 1949, or that the Social Democrats went from 18 per cent in
1946 to 26 per cent in 1947 and then down to 13.5 per cent in
1949. This is some measure of the instability of the era. And, as we
have noted, this period was characterized by a multiparty system of
sorts, with its zenith being reached in the 1947–48 period.

On the other hand, there were elements of stability
even in this period of upheaval and change. Leadership continued
to be predominately conservative (except for the tenure of the
moderate socialist Katayama Tetsu, who had Ashida, the Democratic leader, at his side). Moreover, the conservative leadership,

true to historic Japanese pattern, came from the ranks of ex-officials, in this case the Anglo-American clique of the Foreign Ministry. The real leaders of this period were perhaps the anonymous bureaucrats of SCAP, but the top political figures were Shidehara, Yoshida, and Ashida.

This period, it is true, represented a reign of terror to some conservatives, and, in general, the conservatives' morale was low and their apprehensions were high. But, as we have noted, it was in fact, also a period of conservative dominance, despite SCAP and socialist threats. If one adds Liberal and Democratic votes together, plus those cast for the conservative minor parties and independents, they would represent a rather consistent two thirds of the electorate. As we have seen, the really critical element in the Japanese multiparty system of this period was the Democratic party, especially since the Social Democrats could poll only slightly over one fourth of the electorate at their high mark in 1947.

In the light of the substantial socioeconomic changes and the new political institutions, however, was it not legitimate to ask whether this conservative dominance might be only temporary? After the interval necessary for them to be more fully absorbed, would not the Occupation reforms and Japanese change be translated into even greater political upheaval? One additional factor seemed to make these proper questions. As the first period drew to a close, no party had really succeeded in reaching the average Japanese citizen; all parties remained in some measure exclusive "mutual aid" societies as in the prewar period. Thus the gap between parties and people, Diet and citizen, continued. As socioeconomic change became omnipresent, political change lagged behind.

The basic questions posed above are still legitimate —if largely unanswerable. But the second general era of postwar politics in Japan saw greater stability, not accelerated change. This second era, which began in 1949 and can be considered as still continuing, has been marked by strong conservative dominance and the emergence of a one-and-one-half-party system. Once more, certain broad influences that helped to shape this era must be briefly sketched. In doing this, our purpose is not to present a detailed history of the period, but merely to establish the general context within which Japanese politics have operated since 1949.

Changes in American Occupation policy held a deep significance for Japanese politics in the new era. These changes, as is well known, were closely connected with developments in the world scene. By the end of 1949, half of Asia, whether measured in population or area, was Communist. A complete impasse existed in American-Soviet relations, and the "cold war" raged round the world. Soon that war became hot in Korea, although no direct confrontation of Russians and Americans occurred. The collapse of Nationalist China, the continuance of a divided Korea, and the worsening American-Soviet relations produced many alterations in American official thinking about Japan. The old menace of Japanese militarism now faded rapidly in the American mind with the new menace of communism taking its place. The idea of a weak and pacifist Japan, whose power had been inherited by China, no longer represented an attractive prospect.

Thus American emphasis shifted from punishment and reform to economic rehabilitation, and thence rapidly to proffered alliance. These represent the three basic stages of American policy toward Japan since 1945. The movement into the second stage, as we have already suggested, had important repercussions both within Japan and abroad. In the international arena, American policy was frequently criticized as excessively "pro-Japanese" on such issues as reparations, trade policy, and the entry of Japan into the world community. In the domestic arena, Occupation authorities forged increasingly close ties with the conservatives, who were now firmly in power. It was on the basis of these ties that the American-Japanese alliance began to take shape. The socialists naturally opposed such a trend vigorously. These developments caused foreign policy to become a leading issue in Japanese politics even before the Occupation had formally ended.

We shall examine the central issue of "neutralism" versus alliance in detail at a later point. Here, we wish only to note the political climate in which the debate has taken place. Inevitably, the second general era of postwar Japanese politics has been marked by the rise of nationalism. The Occupation produced its own mistakes, its own contradictions, and in time accumulated enemies of every political hue. But, more importantly, any Occupation reaches a point of diminishing returns rather quickly. To hold the reins of power in a foreign land, and to commandeer the best facilities there, produces adverse reactions before long. Moreover, after a period of intensive "borrowing" from abroad and rigorous self-criticism of most things Japanese, it was natural for the pendulum in Japan to begin swinging back. As in earlier times, the "excesses" of one period led to "corrective" efforts in the next. It might also be argued that the new emphasis upon democracy and individual freedom abetted some forms of nationalist expression.

In certain respects, postwar Japanese nationalism has differed significantly from prewar nationalism in its basic tone and political impact.[16] Naturally, it has been much more defensive, in the manner of the early Meiji nationalist movement. Once again, Japan has been forced to emerge into a potentially hostile world, possessing little strength herself. Once again, the central issue has been how best to protect Japanese security and independence. This time, the external threat comes at least as much from Asia as from elsewhere. The continent of Asia is no longer a vacuum of power. On the contrary, the Sino-Soviet bloc (providing it can remain united) represents the greatest power aggregate that continent has ever held. Consequently, such old nationalist themes as that of a Japanese messianic mission to save the Far East from Western imperialism or communism, along with the thesis of the invincibility of Japan, are now too unrealistic to be advanced seriously, at least in their old forms. Rather, the basic issue has been how to regain —or preserve—an independent Japan.

In addition, postwar Japanese nationalism has served in some capacity as a political weapon for all contenders after power, "left" as well as "right." Before 1945, nationalism was essentially the monopoly of the conservatives. This represented

[16] For two significant English-language works on prewar Japanese nationalism, see Delmer Brown, *Nationalism in Japan* (Berkeley and Los Angeles, 1955), and D. C. Holtom, *Modern Japan and Shinto Nationalism* (Chicago, 1947). On the postwar period, see I. I. Morris, *The Right Wing in Post War Japan,* (London, 1960).

another major obstacle confronting the Japanese socialists, for no political movement in modern Asia has succeeded unless it has been able to capture and use nationalism. In recent years, the conservatives have continued to invoke nationalism in a variety of ways. As the Occupation has receded, they have criticized the excessive "Americanization" involved in many of the postwar reforms. Some fairly basic changes have been undertaken. Even the constitution of 1947 has been under sustained attack from conservative quarters, and efforts to secure various amendments are continuing. The conservatives, moreover, have been deeply concerned about what they regard as a lack of patriotism and a lack of proper ethical values on the part of postwar youth. To correct these deficencies, they have inaugurated various changes, especially in the field of education. As noted earlier, however, the Japanese conservatives no longer have a monopoly on nationalism. In the field of foreign policy, the Japanese "left" have made nationalism one of their primary weapons. The socialists, for example, decry what they regard as the violations of Japanese sovereignty and the pressures upon Japanese decision making involved in current Japanese-American relations. Neutralism is nationalism in foreign policy.

Japanese nationalism thus has new potentialities, and new limits as well. The very fact that it is being used to serve such varied causes reduces some of the dangers present when it was only available to the conservatives and the "further right." Now the various facets of nationalism can be more fully explored, its premises more freely challenged and debated. As nationalism has become a weapon for all elements in political competition, it has been subject to new, often conflicting, interpretations. Perhaps controversy has actually raised the quotient of rationality involved in the use of nationalism by forcing all major parties to defend their position before the electorate. Perhaps, in this sense, nationalism has been made more compatible with demccracy in Japan. Certainly, Japanese nationalism is no longer susceptible to a single image, or even a group of closely associated images. In the process of its political broadening. it has also undergone a process of mutation. Most of the old monolithic qualities are gone or greatly diluted.

Trends in Postwar Japanese Politics

　　　　　While nationalism and foreign policy issues became matters of increasing importance to Japan after 1950, it cannot be said that these factors have occupied the center of the stage. The spectacular economic growth of Japan during the past ten years has been the single most significant aspect of this second general era. The Japanese "great leap forward" began more than a decade ago, and it still continues. In the past twelve years, the gross national product in Japan has increased on an average of approximately 9 per cent per annum. The greatest advances have been scored in industry, especially heavy industry. But agriculture has also enjoyed unprecedented prosperity. As a result of improved scientific farming, increased mechanization, and favorable weather, recent rice crops have been 30 per cent above top prewar production. As already noted, moreover, an increasing number of farm families augment their income by subsidiary work in industry.

　　　　　The result has been a pronounced rise in the Japanese standard of living. Japanese per capita income is still far below that of advanced western European nations, not to mention the United States, but it has been climbing rapidly. Consequently, the domestic market has been greatly expanded. Japan is in the throes of a real consumer revolution. For example, recent surveys indicate that in metropolitan centers, one out of three families now possesses a television set; even in rural areas, television sets are owned by one family out of ten. A multitude of items such as radios and all types of household gadgets have become commonplace. Electrical equipment and farm machinery are also being purchased on a heavy scale.

　　　　　This extraordinary prosperity has affected Japanese politics in a variety of ways. Increasingly, the masses are being caught up in a cycle of very rapid socioeconomic change. Their interests, anxieties, commitments, and energies are increasingly bound up with the issues that stem from that change. These are essentially domestic, practical, and highly personal issues. They revolve around such questions as "Is my job secure?" "How do I get more money to buy the things I want?" and "What chances do my children have?" To some extent, these are the primary questions of modern man everywhere. This era has brought a new commitment to materialism in Japan, however, partly as a result of success, that raises the intensity with which such questions are posed.

The Japanese conservatives have benefited from prosperity not merely because they have represented the government in power, but also because they have been quick to recognize the fact that the average Japanese gives political priority to domestic economic issues. Consequently, they have emphasized prosperity and sought to spell out the future in its terms. Their tactics have accorded with the dominant impulses and hopes of the Japanese people. The socialists, on the other hand, have ignored prosperity, emphasizing a pattern of grievances drawn mainly from traditional ideological sources and spelling out the future either in utopian or apocalyptic terms. They have frequently given foreign policy priority over domestic policy. As a result, they have generally been at a psychological and political disadvantage. Their "idealism" has been posed against conservative "pragmatism"; their pessimism against conservative optimism; their generality (ideology) against conservative specificity (welfare policies). By the same token, however, prosperity can prove to be a double-edged sword to the conservatives. It must be maintained, or they court disaster.

One final aspect of the second general era of postwar politics relates to Japanese reëntry into the world and the search for a *raison d'être*. After 1949, Japan began to reëmerge in the international field from the isolation that had been imposed upon her by defeat. Simultaneously, the search began for some long-range purpose or goal that could utilize the surplus energies and skills of this dynamic society and give it some world status and influence. Both regionalism and internationalism have had a powerful appeal to Japan in recent years. Paradoxically, perhaps, it is this support for regionalism and internationalism today that brings the varied strands of Japanese nationalism, past and present, into closest proximity and harmony with each other. There is an extensive desire to see the establishment of the widest possible network of world contacts and interactions. Such a program is envisaged as meeting two needs: *defense in depth*, the involvement of many states and organizations in various commitments to Japan, and hence the creation of a global deterrent force protecting Japan, having political, economic, psychological, and military components; and, secondly, *expansion,* the export of available Japanese skills, goods, and achievements through peaceful economic and cultural intercourse on an ever broader scale. Through expanded trade and technical assistance, Japan hopes to enhance her own prosperity and perform a world mission simultaneously. The co-prosperity concept, recast in pacific terms, has once again become important. The United Nations has enjoyed enormous popularity. But until it becomes clear that Japan can play a significant role in the new world, restlessness will continue, especially among a younger generation that has been torn from old ways, but not found completely satisfactory new ones. This too has been part of the mood of contemporary Japan, and has been translated into politics.

Against this background, what have been the central trends in Japanese parties and parliamentarism? As noted earlier, two trends have been those of continuous conservative dominance and the development of a one-and-one-half-party system. Since 1949 there have been five elections for the House of Representatives.[17] The first was held in October, 1952. The socialists faced this election as a deeply divided party, actually split into two parties, Right and Left. Thus a further fragmentation of the parties had occurred. The immediate cause of the socialist split lay in the San Francisco treaty. The Right Wing was willing to accept the peace treaty; the Left Wing was not. Neither group supported the bilateral mutual security treaty that accompanied it. Behind the disagreement on foreign policy, however, lay the broad ideological cleavages mentioned earlier.

In the 1952 election, the socialist Right Wing polled 12 per cent of the votes and obtained 57 Diet seats; the Left Wing received 10 per cent of the vote and 54 Diet seats; a group even farther to the left, the Labor-Farmer party, obtained 1 per cent of the vote and 4 seats. The Communist vote, however, was down to 3 per cent (as contrasted with 10 per cent in 1949), and the Communists did not obtain a single Diet seat. If we confine ourselves

[17] See Chart 2 for the general statistics on House of Representatives elections from 1946 to 1960.

Trends in Postwar Japanese Politics

for the moment to the left-wing forces, the election of April, 1953, brought some increases. The Right Wing socialists obtained 13.5 per cent of the vote and 66 seats; the Left Wing received 13.1 per cent and 72 seats; the Labor-Farmer party again got 1 per cent of the vote, and obtained 5 seats; the Communists polled 2 per cent of the vote and received 1 Diet seat. In the election of February, 1955, once again the left increased slightly. The Right Wing got 14 per cent of the vote and 67 seats; the Left Wing received 15 per cent and 89 Diet seats; the Labor-Farmer party got 1 per cent and 4 seats; the Communists obtained 2 per cent and 2 seats. In the election of May, 1958, the socialists, now reunited, polled 33 per cent of the vote and obtained 166 Diet seats; the Communists polled somewhat less than 3 per cent of the vote and received 1 Diet seat. Finally, in the election of 1960, the socialists were once again divided. The left and a major portion of the center, retaining the label "Japan Socialist Party," polled 28 per cent of the vote and got 145 seats; the right forces, led by Nishio Suehiro and running as the "Democratic Socialist Party," got 9 per cent of the vote and elected 17 candidates. The Communists once again polled just under 3 per cent (2.9), and obtained 3 seats.

In this period, three trends can be noted. First, the socialist vote has increased steadily since the dismal results of 1949. Another point, however, must be coupled with this fact. Until the election of 1960, the rate of socialist vote increase had constantly declined. Thus, many analysts saw the socialists approaching a plateau. Could they ever break through the "two-thirds barrier" which separated them from the vast majority of the Japanese voters? In socialist quarters hope was replaced by gloom. As in the case of the British Labour Party, moreover, defeat led to bitter debates over the causative factors. Once again, in the autumn of 1959, the socialists split. This time, however, the split was not even; only a portion of the moderates, mainly the Nishio faction, walked out to establish the Japan Democratic Socialist party. The large majority of socialist Diet members stayed with the Japan Socialist party.

Thus divided, the socialists went into the 1960 election. In terms of total vote, once again the combined socialist factions showed a gain, and, indeed, the rate of increase rose rather than declined. In part, no doubt, this reflected the disastrous finale to the Kishi regime, and the fact that the Democratic Socialists were casting their net somewhat more broadly for voters, albeit with little success. Despite the 1960 results (in which no seats were gained by the socialist parties, taking them together), the united socialist vote remains close to the one-third mark. In addition, the socialists are farther from being united than at any time in the postwar era, although the division is no longer one of equal proportions. On the other hand, it cannot be denied that the total "left" vote in Japan, with one exception, has steadily increased in House of Representatives elections since 1949. Adding left and right socialist groups with the Communists, one obtains the following percentages of the total vote: 1949, 25.2; 1952, 24.5; 1953, 29.5; 1955, 32.2; 1958, 35.5; 1960, 39.2. It is the deeply divided nature of this "left" vote more than its size that casts a heavy shadow over the short-range socialist future.

A second trend interwoven with the first lies in the increasing left-wing domination of the Japanese socialist movement. After the election of 1952, the left consistently polled the larger number of votes and obtained the greater number of seats in the House of Representatives. This trend was indicated in striking fashion in the 1960 election, when the Democratic Socialists polled only 8.8 per cent of the vote and obtained only 17 seats (thereby losing 23 Diet members), while the left-dominated Socialist party polled 27.5 per cent of the vote and won 145 seats (a gain of 23 in comparison with its position just prior to the election). This trend to the left indicates, as we shall later note, the increasing influence of Sōhyō within the Socialist party. It also suggests that the gap between the major Japanese parties has grown wider in recent times, and that the problems of communication between parties have correspondingly increased.[18]

Finally, one may note the impotence of the Japanese Communist party. The 1949 vote, which reached 10 per cent, has

[18] It should be noted, however, that there have been recent signs of a "moderation movement" within Sōhyō and the left socialist ranks. It is yet too early to predict how far this new trend will go.

not been closely approximated since that time. The Communists have obtained no more than two to three per cent of the vote and one to three Diet seats. There are various reasons for Communist weakness. In the first place, the Japanese who wishes to cast a protest vote, or vote "left," has generally had several socialist alternatives. The left-wing socialists, in particular, compete with the Communists on ideological and policy grounds, vying to some extent even for the Marxian label. It cannot be denied that there is a possibility here for interchangeable votes, as well as for Communist influence. In this sense, the potentiality of the Japanese Communist party, especially for infiltration, is greater than appears on the surface, or in terms of its own vote. On the other hand, the Communist party is not popular in Japan, and socialist acceptance of a popular front with the Communists has been remarkably limited, considering the ideological proximities of major elements within these forces. Throughout the recent period, the Communist party has been mainly isolated from the other forces of the left.

There have been many factors involved in Communist weakness, of course. The Cominform attack upon Nosaka Sanzō, a Communist leader, in 1950, gave a profound shock to most Japanese leftists by revealing the party as subordinate to Moscow. Russia has never been a popular nation with the Japanese, and the Soviet government has made no particular efforts to cultivate Japanese support. In fact, its Japan policy has been very stupid from its own political standpoint. And, after the Korean war began, the Japanese Communist party became only quasi-legal. Its main leaders were driven underground, and its communications were disrupted. It has little direct contact with the Japanese people. But the major causes of Communist weakness undoubtedly lie in the popular image of the party as a tool of Moscow, and in the fact that there are alternatives if one wishes to protest.

When we turn to the fortunes of the Japanese conservatives during this period, once again the election statistics provide the most basic data. In the 1952 election, the Liberals equaled their massive triumph of 1949, acquiring 48 per cent of the vote and 240 Diet seats; this represented a decline in number of seats but a gain in percentage of vote, which had been 44 per cent in 1949.

Trends in Postwar Japanese Politics

In the same election the Reform party (Democrats) polled 18 per cent of the vote and obtained 85 seats. At this point, the Coöperative party had ceased to exist. Despite this striking victory, another election was called in about six months. The cause lay within the Liberal party itself. Hatoyama Ichirō, depurged and anxious to become prime minister, challenged Yoshida and sought to build a coalition of factions against him. Despite its huge majority, therefore, the Liberal party became involved in internecine warfare, and Yoshida finally challenged the Hatoyama group by dissolving the Diet and calling another election. Thus the election of April, 1953, found two Liberal parties as well as two socialist parties; on the surface at least, the fragmentation of Japanese politics seemed to be progressive. In terms of results, the Liberal party, Yoshida faction, got 39 per cent of the vote and 199 Diet seats; the Hatoyama faction, 9 per cent and 35 seats. The Reform party continued weak, with 18 per cent of the vote and 76 seats.

For nearly two years longer, the Yoshida government stayed in power, but the cleavages within the Liberal party were never healed. Preceding the February, 1955, election, a new party, the Japan Democratic party, was formed in November, 1954, by uniting the anti-Yoshida forces within the Liberal party and the Reform party. The resignation of Yoshida followed, and in early December Hatoyama, the new leader of the Democratic party, became premier. Thus the Democratic party, based upon a coalition of conservative forces, went into the election as the dominant party. Hatoyama's victory over Ogata Taketora, successor to Yoshida as Liberal party leader, was 257 to 116 in the lower house. The results of the February, 1955, election confirmed the superiority of the Democratic party. It received 37 per cent of the vote and 185 seats, while the Liberal party got 27 per cent and 113 seats.

Following the 1955 election, the merger of the socialist factions took place on October 13, and one month later, on November 15, the merger of the conservatives and the formation of the Liberal Democratic party occurred. These events were widely hailed as the achievement of a two-party system in Japan. At the time of the merger, the Liberal Democratic party had 64 per cent of the lower house membership, against 33 per cent for the Socialists. In the May, 1958, election the Liberal Democrats secured 58 per cent of the vote and 287 seats. Their totals in the November, 1960, election were 58 per cent and 296 seats.

It might also be noted that during the period after 1949 the minor-party vote tended to decline sharply and in 1960 represented less than one half of one per cent of the total vote and 1 Diet member. This was also true of the independent vote in the period between 1952 and 1955, when that vote had declined to 3 per cent. In 1958, however, there was a marked rise, with independent candidates securing 6 per cent of the vote and 12 Diet seats, but dropping again to 3 per cent and 5 Diet seats in 1960. Compared to the first era, the second era of Japanese politics saw a substantial decline in the minor-party–independent vote in national elections.

The general elections for the House of Representatives after 1949 provide an excellent index to the broadest trends in Japanese politics. It is clear that, since 1948, conservative supremacy in Japan has never been seriously challenged by the left. Whether divided or united, the Japanese conservatives have held close to two thirds of the votes and Diet seats. Using Chart 8 (see Appendix), we might also note that the role of the ex-official element within the conservative movement has been increasing. Whereas the ex-officials accounted for 17 per cent of the Liberal party Diet members in 1949, after the 1953 election they represented 25 per cent, and in the unified Liberal Democratic party, after the 1958 election, 26 per cent. The total of former prefectural assemblymen and locally elected officials was relatively stable, being 35 per cent in 1949, the same in 1953, and 34 per cent in 1958. A similar trend was reflected in the Reform (Democratic) party prior to the 1955 merger. In 1947 the percentage of ex-officials had been only 8 per cent, but in 1949 it was 17 per cent, and in 1953, 18 per cent. Locally elected officials and former prefectural assemblymen accounted for 40 per cent in 1947, 39 per cent in 1949, and 32 per cent in 1953.

As we have noted, the Japanese party system went through various fluctuations in the period between 1949 and 1960. At one point, both Liberals and Socialists were openly divided.

Trends in Postwar Japanese Politics

Between November, 1955, and the end of 1959 both parties had healed their cleavages, and this era was hailed as the beginning of a true two-party system for Japan. Actually, it may be doubted whether the new Japan Democratic Socialist party or any other party can attain sufficient strength in the near future to challenge this two-party system. But is it not more accurate to describe the Japanese system as a one-and-one-half-party system? One party remains dominant and always in power. It knows only how to govern. The other is a perennial minority, unable to command more than one third of the electorate. It knows only how to oppose, and at times seems positively afraid of power. Under these conditions, moreover, neither major party is fully dedicated to parliamentarism and its requirements. And both parties remain greatly separated from the Japanese "man in the street." These are some of the major problems confronting Japanese democracy. But to understand the roots of these problems more clearly, we must look inside the contemporary parties.

III

THE INTERNAL
COMPOSITION OF
JAPANESE PARTIES

We have already attempted to suggest certain basic factors about the structure and operation of Japanese political parties. Major stress has been placed upon the leader-follower group, the *faction*, as the vital unit within the party. All Japanese parties are made up of factional coalitions or alliances.[1] Emphasis has also been placed upon the fact that the parties remain essentially closed "mutual aid" societies or clubs, with a very limited formal membership. Indeed, the elected Diet members form the real heart of party organization and control, and if we are to look inside the parties we must discern the trends with respect to this central group.

Consequently, an attempt has been made here to survey certain characteristics of the major-party members of the House of Representatives, based upon the four elections of 1947, 1949, 1953,

[1] See an interesting article by Tsuji Kiyoaki, "I Propose a Multi-Party System," *Shūkan Asahi* ("Asahi Weekly"), March 13, 1960, pp. 6–13.

and 1958 (Charts 8, 12, and 13). These statistics have been combed from the data presented on each member in the *Shūgiin Yōran* ("House of Representatives Survey"), published after each of the foregoing elections. Since in many respects the data is incomplete, the statistics presented here must be used with great care; it is more accurate to assume that at best they disclose trends and tendencies rather than precise percentages. We will note some of the more important omissions as we discuss the data. We have also acquired several lists of the major factions into which the two leading parties were divided shortly after the election of 1958. Therefore, some of our statistics can be broken down into the main factional divisions of the Liberal Democratic and Socialist parties of that period. By this means, a rough notion of the nature of the factions can be obtained.

We must be primarily concerned with the occupational, educational, and interest-group classifications of the Diet members. Reference has already been made to the "ex-official" categories within the major parties, but some recapitulation and amplification may be desirable. First, however, let us define or describe these categories to the extent possible. In general, the ex-officials have graduated from national universities, particularly Tokyo University, before or after which they passed the higher civil service, the judicial, or the foreign service examinations. Thereupon they entered government service, usually reaching the rank of minister, vice-minister, or chief of division within the central government, or attaining the rank of governor (appointed) or chief of division within the prewar prefectural governments. Only after this career did they enter elective politics. Their advantages, of course, include close personal connections with central government officials and the technical experience necessary to participate intelligently in issues relating to their former specialty. In addition, they have usually had substantial administrative experience. As might be expected, these men represent a powerful in-group, or more accurately, a series of in-groups, where intimate connections are often built around school, ministry, and family ties.[2]

[2] For certain recent Japanese studies of the bureaucracy see Fukumoto Kunio, *Kanryō* ("The Bureaucracy") (Tokyo, 1957); Imai Kazuo,

It is difficult to identify the ex-assemblymen and local officials precisely or to give them a clear image, except that they can be considered the heart of the "pure politician" group within the party, as we discussed it earlier. Among the university graduates, those from private universities and colleges predominate, in contrast to graduates from national universities among the ex-officials. Occupational categories tend to be grouped around three areas: the professions, such as law, medicine, and journalism; official service in various prefectural or local interest-groups, including the very powerful agricultural Coöperative Associations, the chambers of commerce, and professional associations; and trade associations, such as those for textiles, livestock, and forest products, among many others.

Generally, ex-assemblymen have been in local politics for some time before ascending the political ladder to the Diet. Thus through their contacts and experiences they reflect local pressures, private interests, and an element of decentralization, in contradistinction to the ex-official group, which tends to reflect the element of centralization and national policy. This latter group is also amenable to private interests, of course, but generally of a more national type, such as the Japan Federation of Employers' Associations.

We have noted that the percentage of ex-officials has always been higher in the Liberal party than in the other two parties, and that this percentage has steadily risen since 1947.[3] In terms of the 1958 elections, 26 per cent of the successful Liberal

Kanryō (Tokyo, 1953); Kanryōsei Kenkyūkai ("Bureaucracy Study Group"), *Kanryō* (Tokyo, 1959); *Kanryō Nihon* (Bureaucratic Japan"), issued by the *Mainichi Shimbun,* Tokyo, in 1956; *Kanchō monogatari* ("Stories of Government Office"), issued by the *Tōkyō Shimbun* in 1958; Naisei Kenkyūkai ("Domestic Politics Study Group"), *Kanryō no keifu* ("The Bureaucratic Pedigree") (Tokyo, 1954); and Tsuji Kiyoaki, *Nihon kanryōsei no kenkyū* ("A Study of the Japanese Bureaucracy") (Tokyo, 1952).

[3] From another source, the "ex-official" faction in the House of Representatives has been given as follows:

2.7 per cent of the Liberal party and 2.1 per cent of the Progressive party in March, 1947

Democratic candidates were in this category. On the other hand, the percentage of ex-assemblymen and locally elected officials has steadily declined, dropping from 40 per cent in 1947 to 34 per cent in 1958. The bureaucratization of the conservative party, as in the late Meiji and Taishō eras, once again has been taking place. This time, however, it could begin from a relatively high base-line. Moreover, Chart 9 shows that the ex-officials have played a very important role in the Japanese cabinets established since October, 1948. It will be noted that a large percentage of the ministerial posts since that time have gone to ex-officials; the figures for the Yoshida, Kishi, and Ikeda cabinets have been particularly high.

It is possible to get a further breakdown of these figures in terms of the major factions which have recently composed the Liberal Democratic party. That party has been divided into eight major factions. Naturally, competition for members among these factions has been intense. There are always some floating or unattached votes, and some individuals who can be bought or won

---

12.1 per cent of the Liberal party and 8.7 per cent of the Democratic party in December, 1947

18.2 per cent of the Liberal party and 12.2 per cent of the Democratic party in January, 1949

22.4 per cent of the Liberal party and 19.3 per cent of the Progressive party in February, 1952

25.7 per cent of the Liberal party and 19.7 per cent of the Progressive party in April, 1953

27.6 per cent of the Liberal party and 18.5 per cent of the Democratic party in February, 1955

The upward trend has been even more conspicuous in the House of Councilors:

8.9 per cent of the Liberal party and 8.7 per cent of the Democratic party in April, 1947

19.5 per cent of the Liberal party and 10.3 per cent of the Democratic party in June, 1950

35.5 per cent of the Liberal party and 29.1 per cent of the Progressive party in April, 1943

38.4 per cent of the Democratic party in July, 1956

The Ryokufūkai ("Green Breeze Society") a second conservative group in the House of Councilors, included 41.1 per cent ex-officials in July, 1956. For these figures see Oka (ed.), *op. cit.,* p. 76.

away rather easily. Treachery as well as loyalty is an omnipresent part of this intensely personal "mutual aid" system. Thus no one can be certain of the exact strength of the various factions, and this will vary from time to time. The leading newspapers, however, have their political reporters keep track of factional strength, and various estimates are given in Charts 10 and 11. The three estimates used in Chart 12 were made shortly after the May, 1958, election by the newspapers, *Yomiuri Shimbun* and *Tōkyō Shimbun*, and by Watanabe Tsuneo, author of a special study of the Liberal Democratic party entitled *Habatsu* ("The Cliques"), published in 1958.[4]

It is most interesting to note that the Kishi, Satō, Ikeda, and Ishii factions had a high level of ex-officials in their group, ranging from about 35 to 40 per cent. The percentage was appreciably lower in the other four leading factions, those of Miki-Matsumura, Ōno, Kōno, and Ishibashi. But in these groups, particularly the Kōno faction, the percentage of ex-assemblymen and local officials was higher. One third of the Kōno faction, indeed, was of this category, with the Ōno and Ishibashi factions just slightly behind this ratio. Only the Miki-Matsumura faction had a low percentage of both ex-officials and local politicians, about 17 per cent and 13 per cent, respectively. On the other hand, the Ishii faction had a relatively high percentage of both groups; ex-officials or former local politicians composed approximately 60 per cent of the total factional membership. The Kishi and Satō factions presented a somewhat similar picture.

The evidence does not indicate that the factional alliances and cleavages within the Liberal party were determined primarily on an ex-official–pure politician basis. Each faction was

[4] Sometimes conservative factions other than those listed in Chart 10 are mentioned. Men like Kaya, Ichimada, and Ishida have their followers. But generally these groups are too small or unstable to be tabulated separately, and they are either considered subgroups under one of the main factions, or are listed in the column "Others." From time to time, of course, the situation changes. For example, the followers of ex-Foreign Minister Fujiyama were originally listed as a subsection of the Kishi faction, but later, especially after the November, 1960, election, this group increased in size and came into its own. Hence, in the two estimates made after the 1960 election, it is listed separately.

itself a mixture in this respect, and other considerations, especially the private deals for personal power, were of greater importance in establishing interfactional alliances. In the Kishi era, for example, the Kishi faction was originally aligned with the Satō, Kōno, and Ōno factions. In 1959 the Ikeda faction replaced the Kōno faction as a part of the Kishi team. Thus the least "bureaucratic" faction within the party was replaced by the most "bureaucratic" one. And these two four-faction coalitions were sufficient to sustain Kishi in office, despite the opposition of those factions left on the outside. The pro-Kishi factions, like all dominant factional coalitions in Japanese politics, were known as the "Main Current," whereas the opponents were designated by the term "anti–Main Current." The distinction between the Main Current and anti–Main Current factions could not be based at any point on the composition of their membership or their attitude toward policy issues. It lay only in their support or nonsupport of Kishi, although some policy differences might flow from this. It is, nevertheless, important to realize that both Kishi and the present premier, Ikeda Hayato, have been leaders of factions in which the ex-official quotient is very high, and are themselves men from an official background, albeit one quite different.

If the Democratic (Progressive) party is surveyed quickly with respect to these same categories, a picture similar to that of the Liberal party is seen. The Democratic party had a somewhat lower percentage of ex-officials and, beginning in 1949, a somewhat higher percentage of Diet members previously elected at the prefectural or local levels. Both parties, however, had over 50 per cent of their Diet members in one of the two categories by 1953. This was a substantially higher total than was true of the Socialist party.

Naturally, the socialists had a small percentage of ex-officials: 2 per cent in 1947; none in 1949; 2 per cent in 1953; and 4 per cent in 1958. The percentage of ex-assemblymen and locally elected officials, however, was high: 38 per cent in 1947; 43 per cent in 1949; 31 per cent in 1953; and 41 per cent in 1958. Whereas only a handful of the socialist members of the lower house have been ex-officials, between one third and two fifths of them have previously held local or prefectural office. Despite their program for nationalization and similar measures requiring extensive support and power on the part of the central government, in reality the socialist Diet members may be more local and sectional in their representation than the conservatives.

Seven prominent factions existed in the Social Democratic party prior to the split of October, 1959. Sources A and B in Chart 13 collected their figures before the split; Source C refers to the period after the split, and hence the Nishio faction here should be read as the Japan Democratic Socialist party. The major socialist factions, reading from "right" to "left," have been the Nishio, Kawakami (so-called right wing), Suzuki (center-left), and Wada, Matsumoto, Nomizo, and Kuroda (left) factions. The Main Current was the Suzuki-Kawakami coalition between 1955 and 1960, although a portion of the Kawakami faction split and went with the Nishio faction to form the new party. Thus previously the anti–Main Current groups came from both "right" and "left."

As might have been expected, the right-wing socialists have generally had a higher percentage of ex-officials and former local officeholders than the left. No faction has had a significant number of ex-officials, as we have previously noted, but close to half of the Nishio and Kawakami factions have been former assemblymen or local officials. Only the small Nomizo and Kuroda factions on the left have approached such high percentages. In general, socialist Diet members have had no experience with the central bureaucracy, but a significant number are graduates of prefectural or local politics. It would be easy, however, to overemphasize socialist "localism." Such tendencies are counterbalanced to a considerable extent by the national-international quotient in socialist ideology, enforced by the prominence of Sōhyō in the contemporary Socialist party.

Turning to the education classification, we have sought to tabulate college graduates among the Diet members, with a subdivision between those from national and private institutions, and a footnote pertaining to those who have received foreign training. Since the conservative Diet members have come generally from the upper social and economic classes, one would expect a high percentage of college graduates, and this is the case. Throughout the period surveyed, approximately three fourths or more of the Liberal party members were university or college graduates. The exact numbers can be seen in Chart 8. This is an extraordinarily high figure in comparison with the educational attainments of the average citizen, revealing the strongly elitist character of the Liberal party. Of special interest, perhaps, is the fact that in the first two elections surveyed, graduates of private colleges out-numbered those from national institutions among Liberal Diet members, whereas the reverse was true after the elections of 1953 and 1958. In 1958, indeed, 48 per cent of all Liberal Democratic Diet members were graduates of national institutions of higher learning. This shift toward national institutions is correlated to the increasing number of ex-officials in the Liberal Democratic party.

When one turns to the eight Liberal Democratic factions (Chart 12), one can see this correlation rather clearly. The factions in which the ex-official quotient is high, such as the Ikeda, Kishi, Satō, and Ishii factions, also have a high quotient of national university graduates, whereas the Ishibashi and Kōno factions have a much higher number of private university graduates. The Ōno and Miki-Matsumura factions are about evenly divided.

Once again, the Democratic party did not show any substantial difference from the Liberals in the educational qualifications of its Diet members prior to dissolution. Both parties had an extremely high percentage of university and college graduates, and in the Democratic party, as in the Liberal party, the trend was toward national university graduates.[5]

The surprising figures relate to the Social Democratic party (Charts 8 and 13). Here one might have expected a sub-stantially lower percentage of university and college graduates, given the supposed socioeconomic base of the party and the heavy role of the labor unions, particularly Sōhyō, in party leadership and organization. However, the number of college and university gradu-ates among socialist Diet members was consistently above 50 per cent, the figure for 1958 being 62 per cent. This testifies eloquently

[5] Among the Liberal Democratic members of the House of Repre-sentatives after the 1958 elections, 90 of the 143 graduates of national

to the important role played by the intellectuals in the party, both those connected with the labor movement and some independent from it. Except for the 1947 elections, a majority of the socialist Diet members with university or college degrees have come from private schools, but the national institution graduates have been nearly as numerous. Tokyo and Kyoto universities, it must be remembered, have long been breeding grounds for left-wing intellectuals. The important point to note is that in educational terms, the Socialist party must be accounted almost as elitist as its conservative counterparts.

Next, let us take up the vital question of economic or interest group affiliations. At the outset, we must warn against accepting too literally the figures presented here. There are many lacunae in the vitas of the individual Diet members. The results

---

institutions of higher learning were from Tokyo University. In the Socialist party, the figure was 21 out of 49.

The following tabulation gives university representation in Japanese cabinets between 1948 and 1960:

		GRADUATES			
CABINETS	Number of members	Tokyo Univ.	Kyoto Univ.	Waseda Univ.	Other universities or colleges
2d Yoshida October, 1948	15	5	4	1	2
3d Yoshida February, 1949	17	4	3	3	4
5th Yoshida May, 1953	18	10	0	2	6
1st Hatoyama December, 1954	18	7	1	5	3
2d Hatoyama March, 1955	18	7	0	5	5
3d Hatoyama November, 1955	19	11	1	2	2
Ishibashi December, 1956	15	4	3	3	4
1st Kishi (Reformed) July, 1957	18	9	1	3	2
2d Kishi June, 1958	18	8	2	1	5
2d Kishi (Reformed) June, 1959	18	8	3	0	6

must be regarded as approximations at best. We shall begin by examining the representation of commerce and industry in the recent Diets. Two categories have been created: first, that of top business leaders, as indicated by the offices of president, member of the board of directors, or similar posts; second, general business affiliation, as indicated by the mention of any connection with a business firm or business interest group. It should be noted, of course, that certain posts, such as membership on a board of directors, are often given to a prominent political figure who is in a position to lend his name and political weight to the enterprise. For our immediate purposes, however, it is not critical whether the business-connected individual be essentially a politician or a businessman. In any case, the above two categories should include all Diet members who represent in some measure the business interest. Unfortunately, it did not seem feasible to attempt an establishment of such subcategories as large, medium, and small business. These divisions, of course, would have made the data more meaningful, and we shall have a brief comment on this matter after the figures have been presented.

As will be seen in Chart 8, over half of all Liberal Diet members have consistently had close business ties. In 1947, 55 per cent held top supervisory or leadership roles as defined above; the figure for 1949 was 61 per cent; for 1953, 64 per cent; and for 1958, 48 per cent. If one adds the other business-affiliated members, the total percentage of Diet members of the Liberal (Liberal Democratic) party who may be considered connected with business was 57 per cent in 1947, 64 per cent in 1949, 67 per cent in 1953, and 52 per cent in 1958. These figures leave no doubt that the Liberal Democrats are predominantly the party of business.

If we turn again to Chart 12, the factional breakdown of the Liberal Democratic party, it will be noted that all of the factions had a high quotient of business-affiliated members, ranging from the Ikeda, Kishi, and Ishii factions, which had over 60 per cent in this general category, down to the Miki-Matsumura and Kōno groups, which had approximately 30 per cent and 45 per cent, respectively. It is interesting to note that the so-called "bureaucratic politician" factions, such as Ikeda, Ishii, and Kishi (Satō is a partial exception), also had the highest "business" quotient. Perhaps a rough distinction should be drawn between "bureau-cratic-business" and "pure business," in the same fashion as the distinction made between "bureaucrat" or ex-official and "pure politician." Since relations between government and business in Japan have been very intimate, the establishment of ties between officials and businesses was a natural development that began in the early Meiji period and, indeed, before. It has been especially pronounced perhaps in the Kantō area—Tokyo and vicinity; Kansai—the Osaka-Kobe area—has sometimes been called the real home of Japanese private enterprise, but one must be careful in making such generalizations. It might also be noted that many Japanese officials have become affiliated with business after retire-ment, in much the same fashion as high military personnel in the United States in recent times. Thus the official or ex-official who becomes affiliated with business through some means may be distinguished from the "pure businessman" whose career has been solely in the business world, irrespective of his connection with, or aloofness from, parties and politics. It might be assumed, for example, that the Ikeda and Kishi factions had a relatively high proportion of the "bureaucratic-business" type, while the Ishibashi and Kōno factions probably had more of the "pure business" type.[6]

[6] Kōno, born in 1898 and a graduate of Waseda University, in his earlier career was a newspaper reporter for the *Asahi Shimbun;* Ishiba-shi, born in 1884 and also a Waseda graduate, was president and chief editor of the well-known magazine *Tōyō Keizai* ("The Oriental Econo-mist"). Other faction leaders coming from a non-official background include Miki, Matsumura, and Fujiyama. Miki, born in 1907, attended Meiji University and studied also in the United States; he was a journal-ist. Matsumura, born in 1883 and a Waseda graduate, was a reporter and member of the Toyama prefectural legislature. Fujiyama, born in 1897 and a Keiō graduate, was a businessman and served as president of the Tokyo and Japan Chambers of Commerce and Industry. It should be noted that business leaders of Japan seldom seek public office for themselves; "pure business" representatives are rare.

In addition to Matsumura, Ōno also represents the "pure politician" type. Born in 1890 and a Meiji University graduate, he was an old member of the Seiyūkai and member of the Tokyo City Council. The

Internal Composition of Japanese Parties

There are some indications that the base of business support for the conservative party movement in Japan has broadened in the period since 1945. In the prewar era, the conservative parties and the zaibatsu were coupled closely in the public mind, and, indeed, the zaibatsu, from all the evidence available, did provide the overwhelming financial support that these parties required, both as organizations and in terms of individual leaders and members. Giant combines like Mitsui, Mitsubishi, Sumitomo, and Yasuda put up the bulk of the funds, not always altogether willingly. The postwar program for deconcentration of business was, as we have noted, abandoned after a rather short period. Some changes, especially with relation to individual family holdings, were effected; at least temporarily, cartels and the larger holding companies were dismantled. Since 1950, however, the great Japanese firms like Mitsui and Mitsubishi have been engaged in a program of reconsolidation and expansion. It does not appear that the structure of Japanese business has been fundamentally altered. Nevertheless, the evidence suggests that today the Liberal Democrats draw funds and support from a considerably larger segment of the business community than was true in the prewar period. There are new and more dynamic business pressure groups than previously existed, providing somewhat broader representation for the business community. This entire question deserves more serious, detailed research.[7]

---

ex-officials include Kishi, Satō, Ikeda, and Ishii. Kishi, born in 1896 and graduate of Tokyo University, climaxed his official career by being a top-level official in Manchuria and then Minister of Commerce and Industry in the Tōjō wartime cabinet. Satō, born in 1901 and also Tokyo graduate, was an official in the Ministry of Transportation. Ikeda, born in 1899 and a Kyoto University graduate, was an official in the Ministry of Finance. Ishii, born in 1889 and a graduate of Tokyo Commercial College, was an official in Taiwan and subsequently chief director of the Asahi Press. It is interesting to note how many of the factional leaders had journalistic experience.

[7] The role of business as an interest group is discussed briefly in a later section. For recent articles in Japanese, see *Shūkan Asahi,* October 30, 1960; Noguchi Yūjirō, "Four Employers' Associations," *Chūō Kōron,* October, 1960, pp. 157–165; and "Japanese Current" in *Sekai,*

Turning to the Democratic (Progressive) party, we see that here also the percentage of business-affiliated members was very high. In 1947, 58 per cent were in the business leader category; in 1949 the figure was 67 per cent; in 1953, 61 per cent. Adding other members with business affiliations, the figures were: 1947, 64 per cent; 1949, 70 per cent; 1953, 61 per cent. In terms of its relation to the Japanese business world, there was no discernible difference between the Democratic party and the Liberals.

What of the Social Democratic (Socialist) party? In 1947, 7 per cent of the socialist Diet members were in our "business leader" category; in 1949, 11 per cent; in 1953, when the party was divided, 30 per cent of the Right Wing and 18 per cent of the Left Wing; and in 1958, 14 per cent. Adding the other members with business affiliations, the figures were: 1947, 31 per cent; 1949, 28 per cent; 1953, Right Wing 35 per cent, Left Wing 24 per cent; and 1958, 18 per cent. One may presume that most of the socialist business "leaders" were connected with small and medium commerce and industry.[8] It has always been recognized that the socialists had a significant "middle-class" vote, and that this vote was reflected in their leadership as well. These figures, however, would suggest that the Japanese Socialist party had a broader socioeconomic base in the earlier period than it had in 1960. Even before the withdrawal of the Japan Democratic Socialist party elements, that base had narrowed considerably, as the 1958 figures indicate. The figures once again highlight the fact that, up to 1961, the party was moving leftward and Sōhyō acquiring greater strength within it.

Examining Chart 13 for factional distribution, we find

July, 1960, pp. 245–249, September, 1960, pp. 62–66, and January, 1961, pp. 235–240.

In English, see Allan B. Cole, *Japanese Society and Politics—The Impact of Social Stratification and Mobility on Politics* (Boston, 1956), esp. pp. 78–89.

[8] For the political activities of small and medium business, see Katō Shimei, "The Political Essence of the Federation of Minor Enterprises," *Chūō Kōron*, May, 1958, pp. 102–108, and Taguchi Fukuji, "Organizational Problems of the Federation of Minor Enterprises," *Annals of the Japanese Political Science Association* (Tokyo, 1960), pp. 64–85.

that, as might be expected, the Nishio and Kawakami factions tend to have the larger quotient of business-affiliated members. For some reason, the left-wing Wada group also has a substantial percentage. Except for the Wada faction, however, the business-affiliated element among the left-wing socialist factions is negligible. Even within the right wing, the current figure is relatively low—roughly 20–25 per cent, and these no doubt, mainly from the small and medium business categories.

A second major economic category is that of agriculture in Japan. As we have noted, approximately 40 per cent of the Japanese electorate may be classified in the rural or agrarian category, although many should be placed in the mixed or "agrarian-related" categories rather than in the "pure farmer" designation. As we have also remarked, the rural vote in Japan goes overwhelmingly to the conservatives. The socialists have not collected more than 15–25 per cent of that vote in the past.[9] But how is agrarian representation reflected in party Diet membership? Once again, we cannot claim completeness for the following statistics; they do, however, indicate the general situation. We have fixed two categories for agriculture, as we did in connection with business. Today, the Agricultural Coöperative Association is a potent organization, both economically and politically. Its branches cover the whole of Japan, and its membership includes the overwhelming majority of Japanese farmers.[10] We have established a separate category for persons designating themselves as Agricultural Coöperative Association leaders. A second category includes persons indicating an agrarian affiliation of any type.

Taking the Liberal (Liberal Democratic) party first, Chart 8 shows that the percentage of Coöp leaders was zero in

[9] For illustration and a more detailed discussion of this point as it pertains to the 1958 election, see Chart 16 and a later section of this work.

[10] For recent materials in Japanese on the Agricultural Coöperative Association see Ishida Takeshi, "An Organizational Study of the Agricultural Association," *Shakai kagaku kenkyū* ("Studies in Social Science") X, No. 4 (1958), 1–66, and Ishikawa Hideo, "Three Faces of the Agricultural Coöperative Association," *Chūō Kōron*, May, 1958, pp. 132–138.

1947; 6 per cent in 1949; 9 per cent in 1953; and 6 per cent in 1958. Adding other members with agrarian connections, the total percentage of Liberal Diet members with agrarian affiliations was 19 per cent in 1947; 17 per cent in 1949; 16 per cent in 1953; and 19 per cent in 1958. These figures may be somewhat low, but the indications are that not much more than one fifth of the conservative Diet members today have their primary affiliations with agriculture. According to its numerical strength, and its party voting record, Japanese agriculture is badly underrepresented at the top levels of the Liberal Democratic party.

Of course, it is misleading to equate this lack of direct Diet representation with political impotence. As we shall stress when discussing interest group–party affiliations, Japanese agriculture constitutes one of the major interest group affiliates with the Liberal Democratic party and contributes enormously to party success. All Diet members representing heavily rural constituencies, whatever their personal occupation or affiliations, will pay close attention to Agricultural Coöperative Association requests and general agrarian interests. Business must still be accorded first place within the party, however, in representation and in power. As the above statistics make clear, it is the one interest group having unequivocal authority at the Diet level. Direct representation and the funds that it makes available for political purposes combine to make this the case. And in this sense, the Liberal Democratic party must be accounted primarily the party of business.

In terms of its factional divisions (Chart 12), the Liberal Democratic party shows substantial differences with respect to its "agrarian" component. Approximately one third of the Miki-Matsumura faction came under this category; the Satō and Kōno factions also had a somewhat higher than average quota of agrarian-affiliated members. But the percentages were very low in the Ikeda, Ishii, Ōno, and Ishibashi factions—factions where the business affiliated element had been high. The Kishi faction perhaps was the most "representative" faction within the party, reflecting the total party distribution and hence serving in some measure as a "balancing force."

Once again, the figures of the Democratic party did

not differ significantly from those of the Liberal party. In 1947, Coöp leaders were 2 per cent; in 1949, 7 per cent; and in 1953, 9 per cent. With other agrarian-affiliated members added, the total percentages were: 1947, 16 per cent; 1949, 13 per cent; and 1953, 14 per cent. Thus we can see that in socioeconomic composition there was never any substantial difference between the two conservative parties of postwar Japan, and hence there were no major barriers to their merger except those of a personal, factional type. The real issue was whether there were enough positions of power to be allotted and who would get them.

Agrarian representation in the Social Democratic party has been as follows: 1947, Coöp leaders, none; 1949, 2 per cent; 1953, Right Wing 3 per cent, Left Wing 6 per cent; 1958, 8 per cent. Adding all members affiliated in some degree with agriculture, the figures are: 1947, 9 per cent; 1949, 4 per cent; 1953, Right Wing 5 per cent, Left Wing 7 per cent; and 1958, 10 per cent. Thus it is to be noted that general agrarian representation in the socialist movement, while it has grown slowly since 1949, reaches only about 10 per cent of the Diet membership. It is important to realize, however, that these figures do not include farmer-union representatives. This "left wing" element has been classified with the Labor group.

In terms of the socialist factions (Chart 13), there are not enough agrarian-affiliated Diet members in the Socialist party to make factional differences significant. As can be noted, the Kawakami faction had the largest number of members connected with agriculture, although the percentages of some of the smaller factions were approximately the same. The important fact is that, if one excludes farmer union representatives, the agrarian segment of Japan is very poorly represented in the socialist movement.

Finally, let us turn to the role of organized labor in the current parties and factions. Once again we have used two categories, of a somewhat different character. In the first category are all Diet members who have affiliations with labor unions. It can be assumed that almost all of these can be classified as "labor leaders," since they generally hold office, either in the national, prefectural, or local unions, in addition to their Diet posts. We have not attempted here to show the subcategories of national, regional, or local union affiliation—a point of some interest and significance. The second category is composed of those who are affiliated with farmer unions. The percentage giving "total" numbers, as in other cases, factors out those with dual affiliations.

It will come as no surprise that the Liberal and Democratic parties have a negligible number of organized labor members (Chart 8). For the Liberal party the percentages are: 1947, zero in both categories; in 1949, less than 1 per cent (one labor-union-affiliated member); in 1953, zero in both categories; and, in 1958, less than 1 per cent (one farmer-union affiliated). The statistics for the Democratic (Progressive) party were only slightly higher. In 1947, a total of 3 per cent (one labor-union, two farmer-union affiliated); in 1949, 3 per cent (one labor-union, one farmer-union affiliated); and in 1953, 1 per cent (one farmer-union-affiliated member).

As the Liberal Democratic party is the party of business, so the Socialist party is the party of organized labor. In 1947, 30 per cent of the Socialist Diet membership was affiliated with labor unions, 32 per cent with farmer unions; the total of union-affiliated members was 52 per cent. In 1949, the statistics were 35 per cent, 22 per cent, and 46 per cent, respectively. In 1953, when the socialists were split, the Right Wing had 32 per cent labor union affiliates, 29 per cent farmer union affiliates, and 50 per cent affiliated in at least one of the two categories. The figures for the Left Wing were 27 per cent, 17 per cent, and 42 per cent. In 1958, a reunited Socialist party showed figures of 33 per cent, 20 per cent, and 50 per cent. One half of the Diet membership of the Socialists comes from organized labor.

Factional differences within the Socialist party—and between the Socialist and Japan Democratic Socialist parties—are not clearly spelled out by our figures. First, we have not distinguished between Sōhyō, the dominant, leftist labor union federation, and Zenrō, the moderate, minority element in the current national labor scene. Today, Zenrō's affiliations are wholly with the right socialists, particularly with the new Japan Democratic

Socialist party, or the old Nishio faction and part of the old Kawakami faction. Sōhyō, therefore, dominates the Socialist party at present, and the great bulk of union Diet members of that party are affiliated with it.

If we look at the socialist factions, using Chart 13, the Nishio, Suzuki, Wada, Matsumoto, and Kuroda factions have the largest percentage of labor-union members. These factions represent the entire ideological spectrum covered by the socialist movement if one omits the negligible Communist party. A more detailed examination, of course, would reveal that Zenrō moderates, many of them older, "pure worker" types, constitute the Nishio supporters, whereas the factions of the left are staffed by younger, Sōhyō members. The Nomizo faction is composed exclusively of farmer union members, with the other factions having about an equal percentage in this category. The right-wing Kawakami faction has a somewhat smaller percentage of union, particularly labor union, members than other factions. In part, this reflects a sizable intellectual segment which, indeed, is spread throughout the party. The Socialists are a single-pressure-group party, but behind organized labor stands the intellectual.[11]

[11] Two other tabulations of socialist composition of the House of Representatives are interesting, and can be compared with ours. The first is given by Taguchi and represents a general occupational breakdown of the socialist members:

	Number of Members		
Occupation	Feb., 1955	May, 1958	
Labor unions	34	48	
Social movements	34	38	(4)
Agricultural relations	20	22	(15)
Middle and small enterprises	20	14	(5)
Lawyers	14	13	(3)
Doctors	9	6	
Officials	8	9	(2)
Journalists	7	6	
Education	4	5	
Social work	1	1	
Other	3	4	(1)
Total	154	166	

Figures in parentheses indicate union-sponsored representatives. See

Internal Composition of Japanese Parties

In official statistics released by the Japanese government it has been customary to present occupational classifications in a somewhat different and more detailed fashion, with considerable emphasis upon "professional" categories: lawyer, physician, educator, and journalist. We also have prepared a chart with the professional categories spotlighted (Chart 15). We would warn against taking either the official Japanese occupational surveys of Diet members or our own chart too seriously. This type of breakdown is likely to be misleading, first, because it is very incomplete, and, second, because it is not possible, on the basis of the information presented, to determine with precision the exact status of the individual *within* his profession. Thus, the term "journalist" covers the position of reporter, but it also includes the posts of editor and publisher. The term "educator" includes ordinary teachers, officials of the Japan Teachers' Union, school administrators, and university professors, among others. We include Chart 15, therefore, to indicate only the rough occupational groupings of the professional members of the Diet, and also as a means of warning against the conventional statistics on Diet members.

Taguchi Fukuji, "A Discourse on the Japanese Socialist Party," *Chūō Kōron,* September, 1958 (p. 127).

The second tabulation is presented by Yanada and gives a general indication of socialist affiliations (including a breakdown within the union movement) in the period between 1950 and 1956:

NUMBER OF MEMBERS

AFFILIATION	Dec., 1950	Dec., 1954		Oct., 1956
		Left	Right	
Labor Unions	3	23	10	31
Sōhyō	...	(19)	(1)	(26)
Zenrō and Sōdōmei	(3)	...	(9)	(5)
Farmers' unions	2	7	12	13
Nichinō	(1)	(5)	...	(6)
Zennrō	(1)	...	(12)	(7)
Other organizations	1	7	9	28
Business	10	4	10	18
Officials	1	2	1	5

Data from Yanada, *Nihon Shakaitō,* p. 142.

There are two final sets of statistics which have some meaning in connection with our survey, namely figures relating to the experience and age of the Diet members. These are to be found in Charts 8, 12, and 13. Both sets of figures might be used to support the general theme of a movement from fluidity toward stability. After the October, 1947, elections, the times the successful Liberal candidates had been elected averaged statistically 2.1; the figure was the same in 1949, but in 1953 it rose to 3.8 and in 1958 to 4.6, indicating the increasing number of Liberal candidates being reëlected. The rise was similar for the Democratic party: 2.2 times in 1947, 2.2 in 1949, and 3.5 in 1953. The socialists started with a lower base and have risen less high, but once again the same trend has prevailed: 1.7 times in 1947, 2.6 in 1949, 3.1 in 1953, and 3.8 in 1958. (See Chart 5.)

The factional breakdowns within the Liberal Democratic party at present are not too significant on this point. The Miki-Matsumura and Ishii factions have the highest seniority in the aggregate, the Satō and Kishi factions the lowest; but the range is only between 5.4 and 4.1. The range within the Socialist party is somewhat greater, from 6.6 for the Kuroda faction to 3.2 for the Nomizo faction. Both of these factions are on the left. The two right-wing groups, however, have relatively greater seniority (Nishio: 5.5–4.2); (Kawakami: 4.4–4.2).

A second factor deals with age. Here our statistics pertain only to the parties as of 1958. After the 1958 election the average year of birth of successful candidates of the Liberal Democratic party was 1901. Five factions, Kishi, Ishii, Miki-Matsumura, Kōno, and Ōno, averaged precisely that year. Two were composed of slightly younger men (Satō—1905, and Ikeda —1902), and one contained slightly older men (Ishibashi—1898). It can be said, however, that the average age of the conservative Diet member today is close to sixty. The socialist Diet member is somewhat younger; after the 1958 election, his average year of birth was 1906. The right wing was generally composed of older men, the left wing of younger representatives, with the Kuroda faction being an exception. As the left-wing segment of the Socialist party has grown, the average age of its Diet members has been reduced. But today it stands in the mid-fifties, which cannot be considered a "young" average.

If for the moment we confine ourselves to the above data, what hypotheses can be advanced concerning the Japanese parties and party system today? Let us start with the Liberal Democratic party—the massive conservative party and the ruler of modern Japan. Today, that party has a relatively high percentage of ex-officials, a percentage that has steadily increased in recent years. Once again, Japanese conservative politics appears to be undergoing a process of bureaucratization, a process that also occurred in the prewar period. Over one fourth of the present conservative members of the House of Representatives are ex-officials, and about 50 per cent of the conservative cabinet members since the July, 1957, reform of the first Kishi cabinet have been from the ex-official group. It is equally important to note that the factions within the Liberal Democratic party which have been dominant in recent years, especially the Kishi, Ikeda, and Satō factions, have had the highest ratio of ex-officials within the party. The ex-official group has not only grown progressively larger, but it has consistently held a degree of power within the party greater than its numerical strength would suggest.

There are also indications that a certain cleavage exists within the party, between its "bureaucrat" and "pure politician" components. The former are closer to the central government and what might be called "national interests," including certain national pressure groups, especially from the business world. The latter, many of whom have graduated from prefectural and local political ranks, are more closely tied to a variety of local pressure groups from the fields of business, the professions, and agriculture. This general conservative pattern, as we have seen, has a deep prewar heritage. At the same time, the factional coalitions are not determined by the ex-official–"pure politician" division. In fact, each faction represents in some degree a mixture. And the decision to join or oppose the "Main Current" is based upon the offers of power and position made to each group. Still, each faction does have certain political proclivities based upon its composition, and

Internal Composition of Japanese Parties

these proclivities cannot be ignored in assessing the political scene. Perhaps one can say that it is these proclivities, based upon the socioeconomic composition of the faction and party, that give Japanese politics its predictability, its stability. And, correspondingly, it is the element of factional division based upon power-position rivalry that gives Japanese politics its fluidity, its instability. This—and the fact that no party has yet really tapped the Japanese people and achieved a mass base.[12]

In terms of Diet representation, business is the predominant influence within the Liberal Democratic party. As we have seen, over half of the conservative Diet members in recent

[12] As we have noted earlier, there are very few independents or minor party members in the national House of Representatives. The prefectural assemblies and the local councils, however, have a much larger independent–minor party composition. Note the following percentage distribution reported by the Local Autonomy Agency:

PARTY AFFILIATION OF PREFECTURAL ASSEMBLYMEN

Year	Liberal	Democratic	Socialist	Communist	Independent minor party
1947	19.7	24.3	16.5	0.2	37.1
1951	41.1	10.9	12.8	0.2	35.2
1955	23.2	22.7	16.1	0.4	38.0
	Liberal Democratic				
1959	60.0		21.1	0.5	18.4

PARTY AFFILIATION OF LOCAL COUNCILMEN

Year	Liberal	Democratic	Socialist	Communist	Independent minor party
1947	2.5	2.9	2.9	0.2	91.2
1951	3.0	0.6	1.3	0.3	95.1
1955	3.7	1.6	2.0	0.6	95.2
	Liberal Democratic				
1959					
City	12.4		10.1	1.6	76.0
Town and village	1.4		1.6	0.5	96.5

The above statistics compiled from Oka, *op. cit.*, pp. 376–377.

years have had their primary connections with business, and no other economic interest group comes close to this strength. Perhaps the professional category should be placed second, despite the difficulty in properly identifying this group. Agriculture would appear to be in a comparatively weak third position. The Liberal Democratic party polls about three fourths of the rural vote, but an overwhelming number of its candidates, even in predominately rural areas, have their main ties with business or the professions. This should not be regarded as startling, of course. It merely suggests that, despite a relatively heavy agrarian component, Japan partakes in the universal urban orientation of modern parliamentarism. To measure merely Diet representation, however, would be to risk underestimating the political influence of the Japanese farmer. Before we define the Liberal Democratic party as a simple single-interest-group party, it would be wise to assess other political factors.

The Socialist party has clearly been an urban party, primarily the party of organized labor and the intellectuals. The new Japan Democratic Socialist party hopes to broaden the base beyond these groups, but as yet it has had no success. This "center" element, despite heavy press support, was crushed in the 1960 elections. In recent years, 50 per cent of the socialist members of the House of Representatives have been affiliated with organized labor. Between 1947 and 1958, business-affiliated socialist Diet members declined appreciably in numbers. The professional group within socialist ranks has been strong, at least on paper. Many elements, however, such as teachers and journalists, are actually a part of the labor movement. It would seem that the Socialist party to a much greater extent than the Liberal Democratic party, is a single-pressure-group party, and its pressure group is organized labor, notably Sōhyō.

The increasing control of Sōhyō ("General Council of Trade Unions of Japan") over the Japanese Socialist party in recent years helps to explain why that party has moved left, when political wisdom would seem to dictate that it move in such a fashion as to appeal to groups like the farmer, the small businessman, and the general middle class. At present, internal labor politics govern socialist party trends. The split between Zenrō ("Japan Trade Union Congress") and Sōhyō and the pressure upon the Sōhyō Main Current (Ōta-Iwai) faction by forces farther to the left are the factors that have governed developments within Japanese socialism. The dictates of internal struggles within the labor movement, more than the dictates of national power, have shaped trends in the Socialist party.

Within the labor movement of Japan, the role of the intellectual is still a major one. The transition toward worker leadership is well advanced, but the tactics, the issues, and the broad ideology of the Japanese labor movement still bear the mark of the intellectual. Only a small part of this group, to be sure, have acted as participants. But they have given Japanese labor its Marxian flavor, its heavy political orientation, its penchant for theory, its ambivalence toward parliamentarism.

The fact that both the major Japanese parties today are in some degree single-interest-group parties contributes in certain respects to political stability. First, within each party, the range of accommodations required on policy matters is not great, especially now that most of the right socialists have withdrawn from the Socialist party. Hence, party positions are relatively stable. Moreover, as long as the parties maintain their present interest group position, there is little likelihood that any shift of political power will occur. The conservatives should continue to dominate the Japanese political scene, provided they are willing to make certain minimal adjustments from time to time and no major catastrophe such as war or depression occurs.

But the Japanese party system represents a paradox, for the element of instability is curiously high. There have been a number of political crises since 1952, of which the recent May-June incidents of 1960 were only the most conspicuous example. In certain respects, the single-pressure-group party system is conducive to instability. It helps to account for the almost total lack of communication between the two major parties, the high degree of class warfare existent in Japanese parliamentary politics. How could it be otherwise, when labor-management relations in the economic field are relatively backward and inadequate? Why should relations in the political field be better?

The politics of Japanese business has never been truly the politics of liberalism. The Japanese business class has not been conditioned to place primary emphasis upon limited government, individual rights, and safeguards for the minority. In the postwar era, especially, there have been some signs of a new progressive conservatism, but its depth and meaning remain in doubt. Hence the tyranny of the majority—or, at least, its indifference to others—is a political factor in Japan with which to conjure. Nor has the politics of Japanese labor been truly the politics of liberalism. The Japanese labor class—should one say, more accurately, the labor leadership?—has not been conditioned to accept parliamentarism as the final arbiter of political issues, or to accept the philosophy that the majority also has rights, including the right to govern.

It is clear that there is a close interplay between the non-liberalism of the Japanese "conservatives" and that of the "progressives." That there is also some relation between the "non-liberalism" of both and the closed party system is equally apparent. It may be questioned whether Japanese politics is yet reflecting adequately the burgeoning socioeconomic revolution that is now spreading across the nation. In Japan, a great new middle class is emerging. But to what extent is it represented in the political arena? To what extent does it really participate? Does not Japanese politics at present tend to represent most strongly the interests of much more limited elements—primarily a segment of business and labor? These are the elements now able to operate as persistent and effective pressure groups, counteracting in some measure the closed organizational character of the parties. But many elements of Japanese society—including a significant part of the rising new middle class—are not yet mobilized in such a fashion as to be capable of operating directly upon the parties. These elements are essentially outside the political process, looking in—and often with the indifference of casual spectators. It is with respect to them that the exclusive organizational structure of the parties operates with particular force.

Thus there are at least three ways in which one can legitimately define the Japanese party system at present. It can be described as a two-party system. Only two parties have substantial Diet holdings. And the Liberal Democratic and Socialist parties are likely to dominate the national scene for the foreseeable future. It is doubtful that the Japan Democratic Socialist party will ever gain sufficient strength to challenge the Socialists, and certainly not in the near future. Other parties, including the Communists, do not count.

It is very tempting, however, to call the Japanese party system a one-and-one-half-party system, as we have suggested earlier. The Socialists are really only half a party, and this was true before the recent split. The Socialists have never been able to break through the barrier that separates them from two thirds of the Japanese electorate. They have been a permanent minority—never really in power and sometimes seeming to be almost afraid of power. Their local and prefectural strength is even weaker than their position at the national level. Their organization exists in only about one third of the Japanese electoral districts. Can they therefore be truly compared with the massive Liberal Democratic party? Japan, like some other so-called two-party nations, has one party that knows only how to govern and others that know only how to oppose. Perhaps this is an ever greater probability in an age when the science of power is increasingly being mastered.

But there is yet another way in which the Japanese party system may be defined. We may consider it a multiparty system, or, more precisely, a system of loosely structured federa tions. Each federation is composed of seven or eight semiautonomous parties. Primary competition takes place among these parties. The activity and energies of the members are largely taken up in this struggle, because it determines the individual fortunes of the members. These parties, of course, are the factions. Factional loyalty tends to become the primary loyalty, being greater than that given the "federation" or any external group. Thus factional strife

—which is continuous—becomes the central source of political instability.[13]

Between the two major Japanese political "federations" there is no real system of communication, as was noted earlier. The process of consensus which governed the methods of historic decision making in Japan (and elsewhere in Asia) is not easily meshed with the majoritarianism which Western-style parliamentarism requires. Between the federations, all is at present either struggle or silence. Perhaps this is of little consequence except to the image of Japanese politics. Up to now, at least, it has not threatened the results, because of the overwhelming dominance of the conservatives. And the real processes of negotiation, compromise, and decision making take place *within* each "federation" as the various parties ceaselessly maneuver in their quest for power. It is here that the volatile and unexpected aspects of Japanese politics exist. It is at this level that decisions vital to the continuity or fall of one administration, questions of a new election, and similar issues are determined.

In one sense, this system provides the necessary flexibility in a situation where the conservatives have never been out of power and the socialists never truly in power. Change is possible and, indeed, is always just beneath the surface. Japanese politics becomes a fascinating, if highly personal, game and one that the people greatly enjoy watching, even as they criticize it as marked by insincerity, opportunism, and venality. The periodic crises and upheavals produce an atmosphere of excitement that obscures in some degree the lack of basic policy shifts and the minimal degree of mass participation.

Thus the Japanese party system is susceptible to vari-

[13] Each faction is organized as a club, with a name such as "Tenth Day Society," "Wednesday Society," or "Wide Pond Society." The factional alliances or coalitions within the party also organize and take a name. For example, in the spring of 1960, the anti–Main Current factions in the Liberal Democratic party bonded together as a society. Lesser combinations are also possible: the Kōno and Miki-Matsumura factions, for example, had a special organization. To cite these facts may give some illustration of the intricate pattern or series of organizations that is involved in such a "superparty" as the Liberal Democratic party.

ous interpretations. In formal terms perhaps, Japan has a two-party system. In broad political terms, that system is really a one-and-one-half-party system. But in the most basic functional sense, it is a system of federations—a system of one dominant federation and one minority federation, with each having multiparties constantly in flux.

IV

THE JAPANESE
POLITICAL PROCESS

We have advanced certain hypotheses concerning the Japanese parties on the basis of general election statistics and socioeconomic data pertaining to members of the House of Representatives in the period 1947–1958. Now, taking advantage of recent research, let us check and amplify these hypotheses by examining recent trends in party organizational activities, interest group politics, and voter behavior.

       When the Liberal Democratic party was inaugurated in November, 1955, it announced its determination to abandon its old position as an elitist party composed primarily of Diet members and to seek a mass base.[1] Two factors prompted this decision. The conservatives had just been through a bitter struggle over the issue

[1] For information on recent developments in Liberal Democratic party organization, we have drawn heavily upon two articles: Takahara Masao, "Organizational Activities of the Conservative Party with Emphasis upon the Shift to Mass Organization," *Shisō,* June, 1959, pp. 91–99; and Adachi Koichi *et al.,* "We Are the Local Organizers of the Liberal Democratic Party," *Chūō Kōron,* April, 1960, pp. 88–102.

of leadership. Yoshida had finally been ousted and his faction reduced to a minority, which was subsequently brought into the new party led by Hatoyama. One of the constant criticisms of Yoshida was that he paid no heed to his party or the public. He was accused of being an anti-party bureaucrat of the old school, arrogant, antidemocratic, and a practitioner of "secret diplomacy" at home and abroad. Hatoyama, on the other hand, symbolized the "pure politician" type of leader, a man who shared policy and rewards with loyal party followers. In the aftermath of the Yoshida era, party organization needed revitalization, and the anti-Yoshida forces had already promised new policies if they were successful. More importantly, the conservatives now faced a Socialist party that had been reunited. Indeed, the conservative merger was an attempt to answer the socialist reunion that had taken place a few weeks earlier. Many conservatives were genuinely worried about the rising political strength of the left. If the socialist tide was to be stemmed, the conservatives would have to pay more attention to their organization and mass appeal.

Consequently, the new party set up a national organization committee charged with the responsibility for developing local party branches as quickly as possible. In January, 1959, in the course of adopting a new organizational program, the party claimed to have made major progress in the first three years. It reported that in the first year, it had established party chapters in 50 per cent of all municipalities; in the second year, it had concentrated upon recruiting young people and women for party membership, and also had established a Central Academy of Politics (Chūō Seiji Daigakuin) for the purpose of training local leaders; and in the third year (1958), it had begun a campaign to reach a membership of five million, launching a system of local organizers that was eventually to encompass the entire nation. In this January, 1959, meeting, party leaders asserted that the Liberal Democratic party already had 2,200 chapters, more than 1,500,000 registered members, including 110,000 young people and women, and 6,100 local organizers.[2]

"Seven great goals" were announced for 1959. These

[2] Takahara, *op. cit.,* p. 94.

included: (1) The strengthening and establishing of branches in all municipalities and *buraku* (hamlets), stimulating membership by offering entertainment and various activities. (2) Increasing and improving local leadership, sending local organizers to the Central Academy for training. (3) Encouraging various political and economic movements—"the people's movement to defend livelihood, freedom, and democracy," "free, democratic unions," and cultural organizations. (4) Strengthening youth and women's organizations, promoting the movement to celebrate Prince Akihito's marriage, coöperation with various youth groups, and the establishment of prefectural student departments. (5) Special emphasis upon the membership recruitment of farmers, fishermen, and those working in small and medium enterprise; concentration upon rural party activities; information meetings with motion pictures; coöperation with the Agricultural Coöperative Associations and "4-H" Clubs; meetings to explain the budget and party policies. (6) More effective, composite campaign policies for both local and Diet elections. (7) Strengthening party morale and consolidating party organization.[3]

In recent years, the Liberal Democratic party has clearly attempted a serious program of mass mobilization going far beyond any previous effort in Japanese party history. What have been the results thus far? According to one source, in early 1960 there were some 13,000 Liberal Democratic party local organizers operating, out of an estimated 20,000 needed to insure national coverage.[4] College graduates were being selected and sent to Tokyo for brief leadership training courses in the Central Academy of Politics. It was the party objective to distribute five or six organizers in each town and rural location, and from twenty to thirty in each city. Such activities as dances, tea parties, and flower-arrangement sessions were being sponsored by local branches to stimulate interest and attendance.

These organizational efforts were being facilitated, moreover, by policies of the national government. In recent budgets, appropriations for public works, social service, and cultural

[3] *Ibid.,* pp. 94–95.
[4] Adachi *et al., op. cit.,* p. 102.

relations have been raised significantly. Through these programs, the faithful can be rewarded, the wayward brought into the fold. Youth hostels have been established and youth leaders sent abroad to international conferences. Women active in party work have been placed on welfare commissions. Employment has been available for those who have rendered service. And the party has never allowed local and prefectural administrations to forget that it is the source of these benevolences.

Despite strenuous efforts and many advantages, however, bona fide dues-paying membership in the Liberal Democratic party has not yet come close to the goals set earlier. Indeed, if Takahara Masao's estimate is correct, it is far below what the party claims. He puts actual membership in 1959 (when the Liberal Democrats were claiming 1,500,000 members) at approximately 300,000.[5] It would seem that the basic problem, to date, has been the fact that most individual Diet members, and especially the leaders of the major party factions, have their own supporters' organizations at the district and local levels. These separate clubs and associations are basically competitive with the regular party branch. Often dominated by local bosses, they are used in local and prefectural as well as in national elections. They may have an aggregate national membership of as many as 10,000,000.

Once again, the primacy of faction over party is revealed. The Liberal Democratic party, whatever the future may hold, derives its present strength mainly from local factional associations rather than from local party branches. While this problem is connected with the whole background of Japanese politics and social organization, the current electoral system helps to support it. It will be remembered that the House of Representatives is elected on the basis of a medium-district system, with three to five members chosen from each district, depending upon its size, and with each voter having a single vote. There is no proportional representation. The candidates having the highest number of votes win.

We have done some research to see how this system affects the Liberal Democratic party factions, using the list of

[5] Takahara, *op. cit.,* p. 95.

faction members prepared by Watanabe Tsuneo. In the 1958 election, conservatives belonging to different factions were successful in 102 of the 117 constituencies into which Japan is divided. A close examination of these contests indicates how intense the competition can be within the conservative party. For example, the third constituency of Ibaragi Prefecture (5 Diet seats) sent four conservatives of the Kishi, Ōno, Satō, and Ikeda factions and one socialist to the Diet. The first constituency of Shizuoka Prefecture (5 Diet seats) sent four conservatives of the Satō, Ishibashi, Miki, and Ikeda factions and one socialist to the Diet.

The fifty-six members of the Kishi faction designated by Watanabe came from 46 constituencies! The forty members of the Satō faction from 36 constituencies; the thirty-eight of the Ikeda faction from 32; the twenty-two of the Ishii faction from 20; the forty-four of the Ōno faction from 38; the thirty-six of the Kōno faction from 35; the thirty-five of the Miki-Matsumura faction from 28; and the fifteen of the Ishibashi faction from 13. Even the faction leaders cannot necessarily control their own constituencies. The first constituency of Gifu Prefecture, for example, elected Ōno, but also elected one member each from the Ikeda and Miki-Matsumura factions, together with two socialists. The second constituency of Hiroshima Prefecture elected Ikeda, and in addition two members of the Kōno faction and one Ōno man.

Under present circumstances, it is not surprising that private political associations provide public party branches with stiff competition. Neither Kishi nor any other prime minister has been able as yet to effect a successful policy for reducing or eliminating the factional problem. Part of the difficulty lies in the complex relations between conservative leaders and interest groups, especially business which furnishes the bulk of the political funds used by Liberal Democratic candidates. To pursue the problem of party organization, therefore, we must look at ties existing between the Liberal Democrats and various national and local interest groups.

To establish accurately the exact cost of current election campaigns or the funds involved in "normal" off-year political expenses for a party leader is virtually impossible. Nor can any reliable figures be obtained on the total amount of contributions of all types. On these matters, however, there have been various educated guesses. Several sources assert that in the House of Representatives election of 1960 Liberal Democratic candidates spent an average of approximately 10 million yen each.[6] The figure estimated for Socialist candidates was 2.5 million yen; for Democratic Socialists, 5 million; and for Communists, one million. If this is roughly correct, the Liberal Democratic party candidates spent a total sum of between 3,500 and 4,000 million yen in comparison to about 1,100 million yen spent by the other parties. This would mean that the Liberal Democrats spent between 75 and 80 per cent of the total funds expended upon the election.

An officially recognized candidate of the Liberal Democratic party receives his campaign funds from various quarters. Grants and "loans" from party headquarters are one important source of money, and toward the end of the campaign an additional "encouragement bonus" is often advanced from headquarters to cover the final drive. But the funds obtained from the candidate's faction leader are also vital. They may well spell the difference between victory and defeat over rival *conservative* candidates. Finally, the candidate relies upon private contributions from various individuals and interest groups, especially commercial or industrial firms with which he has contacts or affiliations, and, in addition, he himself probably contributes from personal savings.

It has been estimated that "financial circles" contributed between two and three billion yen directly to the Liberal Democratic party for the election of 1960.[7] Through what sources was such a sizable fund collected and made available? In the prewar era, as will be recalled, the national conservative parties got the bulk of their funds from a small group of giant combines known as zaibatsu. Then, as now, there were other sources of funds both for the party organization and individual candidates, but in com-

[6] See "Japanese Current" in *Sekai,* July, 1960, pp. 245–249, September, 1960, pp. 62–66, and January, 1961, pp. 235–240; *Shūkan Asahi,* October 30, 1960; and Noguchi Yūjirō, "Four Employers' Associations," *Chūō Kōron,* October, 1960, pp. 157–165.

[7] For instance, see "Japanese Current," *Sekai,* January, 1961, p. 235.

parative terms the zaibatsu role was a decisive one. The Kenseikai-Minseitō was often called the "Mitsubishi party," so close were the financial and personal ties; the Seiyūkai got its support not only from Mitsui, but from Sumitomo, Yasuda, and some of the lesser zaibatsu as well.

Today, the situation has been altered in favor of more extensive and "egalitarian" relations between the commercial-industrial world and the Liberal Democratic party. The postwar era opened with a sharp attack upon the zaibatsu and a serious but short-lived Occupation effort at the deconcentration of Japanese business. Since 1950, the process of reamalgamation has taken place, but there have been other trends as well. In the midst of phenomenal economic expansion, many new sources of power, funds, and influence have emerged, and the party has cast its net wide, to tap these. In part to protect itself from excessive raiding, large-scale business in 1955 created an association to regulate and coördinate its political contributions. This association was given the bland title, Keizai Saiken Kondankai ("Conference for Economic Reconstruction"). The primary function of the "Conference" is to determine the political contributions necessary and desirable (minor sums have also been given to the Socialist and Democratic Socialist parties), to assess members more or less in accordance with their ability to pay, and then to advance the funds to party headquarters. In 1959, when an election for the House of Councilors took place, the Conference reportedly disbursed 740 million yen. In the 1960 election for the larger body, the House of Representatives, the funds advanced were considerably greater.

It is clear, however, that a great deal of money flows from business into politics and political parties through other channels, especially through a vast network of informal and personal connections. The Conference supplies only a part of even the official Liberal Democratic party funds. For example, in 1958 the party reported that it received some 920 million yen for political funds, of which 580 million yen came from the Conference.[8] In accordance with the Political Fund Registration Law, a party must report the amount and sources of its funds at regular intervals.

[8] Takahara, *op. cit.*, p. 97.

These reports do not provide an accurate picture of the total funds actually acquired and expended, but they do suggest the multiplicity of sources from which money is garnered.

Moreover, each faction within the conservative party has at least one organization bearing some innocuous or academic title, the real purpose of which is to collect political funds. Indeed, the strength of a given faction is basically dependent upon the strength of its independent sources of revenue. In periods of crisis, such as when a new party leader is being selected, the major factions may spend millions of yen in various forms of delegate "persuasion." These can be labeled "internal party expenses." But, as we have noted, the size and success of a faction is closely related to the ability of its leader to obtain sufficient special funds so that a strong group of candidates can be underwritten in the highly competitive general elections. Each leader thus has his own connections, sources that contribute specifically to him and his followers. It is reported, for example, that Ikeda's sponsors include the Maruzen Oil Company, Taiyō Fisheries, Yahata Steel Company, and the Toyota Automobile Company.[9]

The connections between Japanese conservatism and business, particularly big business, remain intimate ones. Even a cursory examination of the Liberal Democratic party, however, reveals that interest group affiliation with the party now covers a wide area. Affiliation may involve formal party membership, but not necessarily or usually. Let us look briefly at various types of affiliation now existent. In connection with its drive for a mass base, the party focused special attention upon certain occupational categories that had uniform national distribution and maximum mass contact. Thus today, the party has strong support from groups it has labeled the "seven national mass organizations." These are barbers and cosmeticians, laundrymen and dry cleaners, hotel managers, innkeepers, public bath operators, theater owners, and culinary employees. Most if not all of these groups represent "cluster points" for the society at large—natural centers for widespread political contact. In some cases, individuals from certain categories have joined the party as a group; in other cases, the

[9] "Japanese Current," *Sekai,* January, 1961, p. 238.

affiliation is informal, but this does not make it less meaningful. What *quid pro quo* does the party offer? Primarily, it offers to prepare and support legislation desired by the groups. It may also provide a variety of personal services and benevolences to individuals within groups.

Undoubtedly, the most vital affiliation for the conservatives at the mass level, however, is that with the Agricultural Coöperative Associations. Rapid economic development in postwar Japan has produced a rolling social readjustment. The segment of working population classified as "agrarian" was reduced from 47 per cent in 1948 to 36 per cent in 1958. Of at least equal significance is the fact that those agrarian households having non-agricultural workers increased from 45 per cent in 1947 to 62 per cent in 1955. On the other hand, regular workers and apprentices increased from 17 per cent of the working population in 1948 to 26 per cent in 1957, and those engaged in tertiary or service industries rose from 23 per cent in 1948 to 36 per cent in 1957. These are only the most obvious effects of a rapidly accelerating industrialization.

Despite their numerical decline and the infiltration of nonagrarian elements into their midst, however, Japanese farmers are still a supremely important political bloc for the conservative cause. They continue to represent the largest single socioeconomic category of voters by a considerable measure. There are two factors, moreover, that add weight to their numerical strength. The percentage of eligible voters who vote is much higher in rural than in metropolitan areas, as we shall note later. In addition, the present distribution of districts for the House of Representatives greatly favors the rural voter. A recent government survey based upon the October 1, 1960, census indicated that each representative in the lower house of the Diet should represent numerically 200,015 persons. In fact, however, one lower house seat represented as much as 300,000 persons in some metropolitan constituencies, whereas in various rural areas, the ratio was only 150,000 persons to one seat.[10]

[10] For a report on this survey see the New York *Times,* February 7, 1961. See also Shimizu Keihachirō, *Sengo Nihon no sōsenkyo no jittai* ("The Actual Conditions of the General Elections in Postwar Japan")

In postwar Japan, the most important rural organization without question has been the Agricultural Coöperative. Cooperatives have been established throughout the nation and have an almost universal farmer membership. In large measure, they control economic and social activities in the Japanese rural areas and maintain the extrarural economic ties. Politically, the Coöperatives are closely affiliated with the Liberal Democratic party. Every survey has indicated that the great majority of Coöperative leaders actively support the party.[11] Indeed, they are frequently called its "standing organizers." At a later point, we shall discuss in somewhat greater detail various factors involved in the capacity of the conservatives to hold the rural vote in Japan. Here, we shall only note that the Coöperatives are symbolic of the new, mass-based interest groups that have developed in the postwar period. They play a major role in both the selection and the support of conservative candidates from predominantly rural areas. Agrarian affiliation with the Liberal Democratic party is most meaningful in terms of the bulk vote that it represents, but it also has financial implications. A counterpart exists in agriculture to the Conference for Economic Reconstruction, namely, the Nōgyō Mondai Kenkyūkai ("Agricultural Problems Research Association"). Operated by leaders of various agrarian organizations, this association collects and disburses campaign funds.

Once again, what are the services rendered by the

(Tokyo, 1959); and the *Asahi Journal,* October 16, 1960. According to Shimizu, the current constituency system, established in 1950, was based upon the 1946 census. Since that time, the population of Tokyo and other large cities has increased rapidly. In 1959, in the first constituency of Tokyo, one seat represented 240,000 people, or three times more than the 78,000 people represented by one seat in the Hyōgo fifth constituency or the Ibaragi second constituency.

[11] Takahara, *op. cit.,* pp. 98–99. Reportedly, in Aichi and Miyazaki prefectures in 1959, 64 per cent and 51 per cent, respectively, of the Agricultural Coöperative heads supported the conservative party; 33 per cent and 46 per cent had unknown political affiliations; and 3 per cent in each case supported the Socialist or Communist party. See Sakurai Makoto, "This Is the Way the Agricultural Coöperative Heads Think," *Nōkyō* ("The Agrarian Coöperative") August, 1959.

party in exchange for this aid? In the field of domestic policy, many issues are of direct concern to the farmer. Each year the government fixes the price of rice, determines support for agricultural research, and legislates a public works program. On these and many other issues the Liberal Democratic members of the Diet pay careful heed to agrarian interests. Fortunately for the conservatives, economic conflict between agrarian and commercial-industrial interests is minimal in Japan, in comparison with most modern societies. Nearly 80 per cent of all industrial raw materials must be imported, so the possibility of conflict in this area is limited. Japanese agriculture does not depend upon hired labor. Nor is there any troublesome agrarian surplus to push prices down; only a labor surplus that industry must absorb. Moreover, the Occupation conducted a drastic land reform that greatly reduced agrarian debt and urban financial controls. Thus it is possible for the Liberal Democrats to serve commerce and industry on the one hand, and agriculture on the other, with relatively minor difficulties and contradictions, especially in recent years. Japanese rural society has taken on an increasingly mixed socioeconomic character as a result of heavy industrial-commercial penetration, and hence the cultural disparity between rural and urban life has been lessened. In terms both of the composition of its elite and its over-all operational priorities, the Liberal Democratic party is preëminently the party of business. But its mass foundations—its majorities—are strongly dependent upon the farmer. It cannot afford to forget this fact.

Under present circumstances, however, the Liberal Democrats constitute a permanent governing party, and this gives them a signal advantage in attracting interest groups. Now and for the foreseeable future, this is the party with national funds, legislation, and power to distribute. The list of groups affiliated with the conservative party is a lengthy one. It includes such groups as the Japanese Medical Association (claiming 70,000 members), the League of Repatriates from Overseas (claiming 3,000,000), the Japan Veterans Association (claiming 1,500,000), the Japan Association of Families Bereaved by the War (claiming 1,700,000 households), the Political League of Small and Medium Enterprises (claiming 700,000 firms), and the Sōka Gakkai (a new religious sect claiming 1,200,000 members). Needless to say, there is much overlapping of membership among the groups affiliated with the Liberal Democratic party, and no group can commit its members fully to party support; however, the network of ties between national interest groups and the conservatives is both impressive and effective.

The dominant position of the Liberal Democratic party in government also strengthens party influence with local and prefectural administrators, and with the whole of the civil service. As is well known, government in Japan remains highly centralized. The finances of local government are heavily dependent upon the national budget, and local administration is supervised and regulated in a multitude of ways by the national government. The conservatives, continuously in power at the national level, have not only developed close working relations with local and prefectural elected officials in most cases; they have also made it clear to all concerned that the election of socialists might hamper the flow of funds and services. Of equal importance is the fact that at every level, the conservative party has penetrated the civil service to a degree unprecedented in the past. Postmasters are active on behalf of the Liberal Democratic cause. Prefectural appointees work closely with the regional party organization. Foreign Office men frequently rely upon political ties for choice assignments.[12] Patronage has become another major conservative weapon.

In sum, conservative dominance in Japan is the product of a triple alliance between the bureaucracy, key national interest groups, and the Liberal Democratic party. We noted earlier in terms of Diet membership that there has been a progressive bureaucratization of the conservative party. But one might also say that there has been a progressive party infiltration of the bureaucracy. Interaction at all levels—local, prefectural, and na-

---

[12] Here also, however, factional alignment sometimes causes complications. Japanese political observers have noted that on occasion, intimate communication between the prime minister and an ambassador in a prominent foreign post has been hampered by the fact that the ambassador is associated with a rival faction within the Liberal Democratic party.

tional—has produced a degree of party-bureaucratic intimacy unparalleled in Japanese history. Our survey of lower house members
indicated that the number of direct, personal ties between the
working politicians and the commercial-industrial world has been
striking, equaling or exceeding 50 per cent of the total house
membership. We know the chief reason for these ties: the need for
vast amounts of political funds. But the primacy of business as an
interest group in Japanese politics is not to be construed as meaning
that business holds exclusive prerogatives. The commercial-industrial interest group can deliver money, but it cannot deliver masses
of voters, and the days of old-fashioned vote buying are almost
over. The mass element must thus be supplied from other sources,
and to obtain this, the Liberal Democratic party has not only
launched a campaign since 1955 for a nationwide organization
with mass membership—it has also sought to build or strengthen
its affiliation with various nationa¹ interest groups. These affiliates
cover a broad spectrum of Japanese society: agriculture, the voca-
tional trades and service industries, small and medium business,
selected professions, and the nationalist-patriotic front.

This is a formidable combination for power, even if
its votes cannot be solidly delivered. Yet, the evidence also shows
that the Liberal Democratic party faces real problems. In various
respects, our earlier hypotheses about the nature of the Japanese
party system have been bolstered. Most indications are that, barring
some major depression or similar catastrophe, the conservatives
will continue to be the government. For the near future at least, the
one-and-one-half-party system will prevail. But the central question
remains. Do the Liberal Democrats represent a party, or are they
a federation of parties? Serious attempts to create a mass-based
party organization have been under way since 1955. Perhaps these
attempts will ultimately succeed. Some gains have been scored. Up
to date, however, efforts for such an organization have been frustrated to a considerable extent by the numerous sizable "supporters'
organizations" whose members pay allegiance to a faction or individual. These associations are much stronger than local party
branches. It is in lieu of strong organization at the grass roots, in-

deed, that the party must be dependent upon its national interest group affiliates. But here also the factional ties are often the crucial ones. Competition within the party is fierce, both at election time and in the interim periods. Victory generally goes to the faction that can build the strongest independent base of boss, interest group, and financial support.

What of the Socialist party? In recent years, the Socialist party has talked at length about the need for a revitalized organization. The old cry, "To the masses!" is constantly reëchoed. Only 30 per cent of the Japanese workers are unionized, it is asserted; the remainder must be tapped and instilled with class consciousness, especially those in small and medium industry. Nor should the farmer be allowed to go to the conservatives by default, it is argued. "A day-by-day concern for his problems," new policies for the Coöperatives, and other overtures to the rural voter have been urged. The Socialists have also talked about giving more attention to the middle class, a group from which they already draw support.

In 1957, in an attempt to realize some of these objectives, the Socialists launched a widely heralded new organizational campaign. The central executive committee was authorized to appoint central and local organizers in order to recruit members and establish additional ties with mass organizations. There were four initial goals: expansion of party membership to at least 100,000; the conversion of "candidate-oriented supporters" to "party-oriented friends"; the use of activists to expand party influence over the "unorganized masses"; and the strengthening of ties between the party and mass organizations, especially the trade unions and farmers' associations. Two methods were advanced to accomplish this latter goal: the recruitment of "supporting organizations" and the establishment of party units within a union or other external body.

Despite these efforts, however, the Socialist party remains, in the words of one observer, a "ghost party," a loose combination of candidates and their supporters or supporting groups, with each candidate going his own way when the election starts.[13] By 1959, eight central organizers and 158 local organizers had been appointed. The party aimed at the placement of five regional organizers in each prefecture. But the organizational campaign has definitely faltered, up to now. At the time of the 1960 election, party membership did not exceed 60,000, with only 5,000 to 10,000 "active members." [14] Somewhat earlier, at the time of the 1958 general convention, 1,320 party branches were reported, including some special district and factory branches scattered among the 4,104 political subdivisions of Japan. Thus the party has an organization in less than one third of the subdivisions, although such an organization requires only thirty members in the case of cities and twenty in towns or rural districts. Approximately

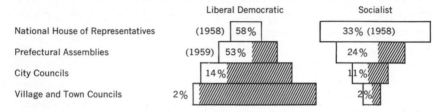

	Liberal Democratic	Socialist
National House of Representatives	(1958) 58%	33% (1958)
Prefectural Assemblies	(1959) 53%	24%
City Councils	14%	11%
Village and Town Councils	2%	2%

Liberal Democratic and Socialist political strength as measured by percentage of seats held in elective office. Shaded areas represent independents affiliated with, or commonly associated with, the respective parties.

3,000 political subdivisions have no Socialist organization, the rural areas representing especially barren ground.

It is not surprising, therefore, that while the political

[13] Taguchi Fukuji, "A Discourse on the Japanese Socialist Party," *Chūō Kōron,* September, 1958, pp. 125–126.

[14] Taguchi Fukuji, "A Discourse on the Japanese Socialist Party," *ibid.,* February, 1961, p. 29.

There were approximately the same number of members in May, 1958. At that time, a breakdown of the membership revealed the following facts, in terms of age composition: 22 per cent of the members were between twenty and thirty, 29.8 per cent between thirty and forty, 23.4 per cent between forty and fifty, 14.5 per cent between fifty and sixty, and 4.3 per cent sixty or over. By occupation 52.7 per cent were industrial workers and 23.5 per cent were engaged in agriculture or fishing. See Hisayoshi Takeo, "The Organizational Power of the Progressive Parties," *Shisō,* June, 1959, pp. 82–90.

strength of Japanese conservatism can be depicted by a pyramid, with its broad base resting in the rural districts, the political strength of Japanese socialism must be represented by an inverted pyramid, its greatest support coming at the national level.

Why has the Socialist organizational effort proved abortive thus far? Many causes are involved; doctrinal divisions, financial limitations, weak leadership, and inexperience are continuing troubles. But, once again, the problem of factionalism and the nature of the dominant interest group that sustains it have contributed mightily to the failure. When the party pledged itself to the recruitment of "supporting organizations," it defined these as groups approving the program and the policies of the party and in which more than one third of the officials were party members. If the supporting organization covered more than one prefecture, it was to be attached directly to party headquarters; otherwise, it was to be tied into the prefectural party office. By mid-1959 there were twelve organizations attached to headquarters, with a total membership of 824,000; almost all were labor unions.[15] In addition, unions having some four million members coöperated with the party prior to January, 1960, when Zenrō, with a membership of between 800,-000 and one million, broke away to support Nishio's Democratic Socialist party.

Organized labor is thus the major interest group closely affiiliated with the socialists. Within organized labor, Sōhyō, with its 3,500,000 members, dominates both the labor scene and the Socialist party. Its organization serves as a substitute for the weak party organization. Its finances and campaign work have become almost indispensable to the success of any socialist candidate. In many areas where the Socialist party does not have a branch, local units of Sōhyō—such as the communications workers', railway workers', and teachers' unions—provide facilities, campaigners, and candidates. In its financial relationship to the Socialist party, Sōhyō occupies a position similar to that of the Conference for Economic Reconstruction in the Liberal Democratic party. While its contributions are much smaller than those of big business, Sōhyō is the one major source of financial support for the

[15] *Ibid.,* p. 84.

Socialist cause. Union leaders, most of whom are party members, play a leading role in determining union-party relations, selecting party candidates, and allotting financial support. How critical union support has become is illustrated by the following statistics: in the election of 1958, 73 per cent of all candidates sponsored by Sōhyō unions were elected, 68 per cent of those sponsored by Zenrō unions, and 84 per cent of those jointly sponsored. When this winning record is contrasted with the generally dismal results obtained by Socialist candidates who are not sponsored, the rising power of the unions within the Japan Socialist party can be understood.

The union movement itself, however, is badly fragmented. Well known is the division between Sōhyō, the left socialist federation in which government employee unions predominate, and Zenrō, the right socialist federation composed largely of private industry workers like the textile workers and seamen. The entire union system, however, is based upon the individual enterprise or plant local. The various enterprise unions are then affiliated on an industrial basis into regional and national organizations. Sōhyō is a rather loosely constructed federation of such national organizations, themselves often called federations. But the basic unit remains the enterprise union at the local level and the enterprise-wide federation at the regional or national level. This fact represents one basis for factionalism both within the unions and within the Socialist party. Union candidates for the Diet are sponsored either by an enterprise local or by some all-industry federation. The bulk of funds and campaign support comes from this single source. If the candidate is successful, he is likely to become a "special interest" representative, beholden to this constituency. Naturally, therefore, factional conflicts within the labor movement, even within Sōhyō and Zenrō, have a direct impact upon the socialist parties.

Other than from organized labor, neither of the present socialist parties has been able to garner affiliates having organization, funds, and mass support. For their votes, as we shall note later, the socialists have counted heavily upon the middle and lower-middle economic groups. They have drawn a substantial vote from such diverse groups as the technician and white-collar classes, the skilled and semiskilled workers, the intellectuals, and even some of the small and medium entrepreneurs. The socialist parties, however, do not have the interest group aggregate possessed by the conservatives, and that is one basic reason, of course, for their minority status. The socialists do have some advantages in the field of mass media communications. While radio and television are relatively neutral, the press has often leaned toward the opposition in criticizing the government in power, and the press has a huge audience in Japan.

Nevertheless, both the Socialist and the Democratic Socialist parties are essentially cadre or "Diet membership" parties at present. The factional composition of the parties is influenced by various factors. We have already mentioned the new type of union-sponsored Diet member. Conflict may exist not only among this type when rival unions or federations are involved, but also between the union-sponsored and the "pure party" type of socialist representative. There is also a generational difference that is increasingly important, a difference between the prewar veterans and the postwar "newcomers" who are now in the process of taking over the party reins.[16] Interactive with these and other factors are the ideological variations that extend over a wide range, from orthodox Marxism to Fabian socialism. Nor was this range narrowed within the Socialist party because of the defection of the Democratic Socialists. Some Fabians stayed with the left wing for personal, political, or other motives.

Factionalism within the socialist movement, even with-

[16] For a discussion of these various factors, see Taguchi, *op. cit.,* September, 1958, pp. 128–129. Taguchi states that the veteran prewar proletarian party group is known by the nickname *koseki* (the official census register wherein one's birthplace and date are recorded) while the postwar group is labeled *buraku* (the hamlet or small cluster of houses that comprises the basic unit of Japanese rural settlement).

Taguchi also notes that there is a certain element of conflict or policy difference between the Diet members and the young secretary-managers who man the headquarters and branch offices. The former think primarily in terms of a Diet-centered party and are very conscious of their own prestige. The latter agitate for party rejuvenation and emphasis upon a mass base.

in the present Socialist party, thus rests upon a very complex set of factors. In part, it is the product of deeply rooted cultural forces that contribute to a "Japanese-type organizational model," a structure built on the basis of loosely federated leader-follower, familial-type units. This heritage the Socialists share with all other groups in their society: trade union, conservative party, business association, and university. In addition, however, many other factors contribute to the incidence and form of socialist factionalism: the special characteristics of Japanese unionism and the Japanese intelligentsia, and the unique transitional relation currently existing between historic and contemporary forces in Japanese socialism as seen in differing models of leadership, ideology, and organization.

As in the case of the Liberal Democratic party, the record of Socialist organizational efforts tends to validate the theories set forth on the basis of our historical research and our survey of contemporary members of the House of Representatives. Compared with the prewar period, the Japanese socialist movement has made substantial gains in less than two decades. If its uneven, sharply torn pieces are put together, they total somewhat over one third of the popular vote and the lower house seats. Yet when one examines the present party affiliate combinations, the sociopolitical base of the Japanese one-and-one-half-party system is made clear. The conservative majority is based upon the tripod of bureaucracy, multiple interest-groups, and a network of party branches and "supporter organizations" servicing individuals and factions within the party fold. The socialist minority is based upon an almost total absence of official support from local, prefectural, or national administration and has a more restricted interest group affiliation, which in turn effects the strength and character of party branches and "supporter organizations."

In both cases, primary party organization is weak. This is especially true of the Socialist party. Perhaps one should not overemphasize the matter of membership. In British political parties, for example, card-carrying party members are not numerous. More important, undoubtedly, is the competition within and surrounding the party organization, and the question of public identification with parties. In large measure, the organizations established to support factions, sustained by the same interest-groups, compete with the Liberal Democratic party for power, funds, and public prestige. At the local levels, particularly, they often receive more attention and support. *They* are the party. Similarly, such organizations in the socialist camp, created from within organized labor, are competitive with the party and usurp powers which should lie with the party powers. To the extent that the factional or individual organizations are private, closed groups, they blur the image of the party as a public, open association. To the extent that they are open, they serve as primary groups, relegating the party to secondary status. All of this serves to weaken public identification with and commitment to the major parties.

Perhaps the quotient of modernity in Socialist factionalism is higher than that in Liberal Democratic factionalism—that is, factors such as ideology, policies, and political tactics may play a larger role in producing socialist divisions, and factors of personal allegiance or provincialism a smaller role. Yet, for both parties this is a confusing, transitional era in which new qualities derivative from the rapid advent of Japan as a mass society are vying with qualities carried on from the premodern period. One might characterize the current Japanese parties as symbols of the ongoing, progressive interaction and intermingling of "massification" and "exclusivist" properties. It is vitally important that the parties be seen as a part of a process rather than merely as a structure, so that we can move away from the false image of a relatively static, relatively contained, separate institution and capture the full sweep of movement, synthesis, paradox, conflict, and growth that preoccupies Japanese politics today.

To relate the parties to the political process, it is important first to look briefly at Japanese voting behavior. We shall concentrate here on elections for the House of Representatives, for this is the basic determinant of national party strength. The formal campaign for Diet elections is relatively short, the election taking place within a month of Diet dissolution. To become a candidate is not difficult. The individual need only be a native-born Japanese citizen, twenty-five years of age or older, file simple election papers with the local election board, and put up a deposit of 100,000 yen.

The Japanese Political Process

This deposit is returned if he polls at least one fifth of the total vote in his district, divided by the number of seats to be filled. More complex and more important is party endorsement. Every party has an election committee entrusted with the difficult task of authorizing the party slate in each district. Factional pressures operate here intensively, and important matters relating to political tactics must be resolved. Only the Liberal Democratic party has the funds—or the political basis—to run close to a full slate of candidates. Generally, the socialist parties have run an insufficient number of candidates to obtain power, even if all their candidates won. (See Chart 4.) This situation is dictated not by a paucity of available candidates, but by the knowledge that it is futile to spread political funds too thin, and with the recognition that, in most districts, if any victory is to be scored all socialist votes must be cast for one candidate, or be divided among no more than two or three. But who runs, and in which district, can have a powerful influence upon the various factions within both major parties. The election committees decide this formally, but the amount and location of the funds, the pattern of local support, and the balance of factional and personal pressures create the climate for the decisions.

Cognizant of the massive corruption that characterized elections before World War II, Occupation and Japanese authorities have fashioned postwar election rules that are unusually strict.[17] Various groups, including police, judges, civil service officials, schoolteachers, and minors, can take no part in election campaigns. Party and individual expenditures are limited by law. Both funds received and expenses must be reported. There can be no door-to-door soliciting of votes and no gifts of food, drink, or money by the candidates. No more than sixty individual campaign speeches may be given, but each candidate must attend a series of joint candidate meetings sponsored by the local election-supervision commission. Campaign parades and demonstrations are banned, and various other techniques are regulated.

Every attempt has been made to cut the costs of campaigning, and to insure that necessary facilities shall be free

[17] For a detailed discussion of election regulations see Yanaga, *Japanese People and Politics,* pp. 286–290.

and equal. Each candidate presents a brief statement and personal vita. These are printed by the prefectural election-supervision commission in the form of an election brochure which is distributed free of charge to all voters in each election district. Each candidate is also given an equal amount of radio time in which to present his personal qualifications and political views; he is not allowed to have additional time, even at his own expense. Each candidate is also given a small newspaper advertisement and a specified number of postcards, posters, and banners. He is, finally, presented with a stipulated number of railway and bus passes for his campaign transportation.

These are the rules. What are the practices? In spite of the assistance provided in the form of free facilities, and the limits imposed upon funds and methods of campaigning, Japanese elections continue to be extremely costly, as we have noted earlier. In most cases, the heaviest expenditures are those that go to a candidate's network of local bosses, "ward leaders," and prominent supporters. Some of these men are themselves officeholders—mayors, prefectural assemblymen, or local councilmen. Others are men of influence because of their family, their positions, or their connections. Still others are, in effect, professional election brokers. All supposedly have one thing in common: they can deliver a certain number of votes. The funds transmitted to them are used in a variety of ways—for themselves, for their group, or for their general "sphere of influence." The more men of this type that a candidate can obtain—perhaps one should say, can afford—the better his chances of election naturally become. These men constitute the base of his personal *jiban,* or constituency support. Traditionally, their influence was easily discernible because the average candidate would receive his votes in scattered blocs where his *jiban* was strong, rather than in any uniform fashion throughout the district.[18] In these respects also, a transition is now under way.

[18] For a discussion of *jiban* and other aspects of the Japanese election system, see Junichi Kyōgoku and Nobutaka Ike, *Urban-Rural Differences in Voting Behavior in Postwar Japan* ("Stanford University Political Science Series," No. 66), reprinted from *Proceedings* of the Department of Social Sciences, College of General Education, University of Tokyo, 1959.

Gradually, personalized *jiban* is being broadened into a modern, less stable, but more intensive political organization, especially in urban centers.

Today, in many constituencies, there are fewer fixed boundaries and sources of personal support. Each candidate must campaign more vigorously in person. The standard campaign techniques are the use of a sound truck or auto, blaring out the candidate's name and a few brief remarks; the street-corner speeches; the sponsored meetings, and the use of mass media in the fashion prescribed by law. But there is also a great deal of quasi-legal and illegal activity. Direct vote buying is no longer a common practice, but, in Japan as elsewhere, it is difficult to draw the line between bribery or vote buying and the transmission of various gifts, favors, and entertainment. Nor is campaigning confined to the formal election period. Increasingly, the successful Japanese politician must provide a continuous flow of benevolences, stepping these up as election time draws near.

Japanese elections, however, do not take place without debate on substantive issues. At present, as we have noted, the overwhelming majority of candidates run under a party label, most of them running under the label of the Liberal Democratic or Socialist parties. The leaders of these parties now conduct nationwide speechmaking tours, and also use the mass media to the fullest possible extent. At election time, more than at any other period, the parties tend to project some image—especially the conservatives, who have the prime minister as spokesman. What have been the dominant themes set by national party spokesmen in recent elections?

The Liberal Democratic party has naturally placed heavy stress upon domestic economic issues. They have run repeatedly on a platform of "prosperity and progress." Not only have they claimed credit for the economic boom of the past decade, but they have promised to continue and expand Japanese economic growth. In the campaign of November, 1960, Ikeda and the other conservative leaders spelled out a program to double production in ten years, achieving complete employment and a standard of living equal to that of the West. They promised that the nine per cent annual increase in gross national product would be maintained; that prices would be kept stable by increasing production or liberalizing imports; and that utility costs, service fees, and taxes would be maintained at the present level if at all possible. In addition, a substantial expansion of public works in housing and roads was indicated; along with increased social security. In certain respects, the Japanese conservatives have moved unabashedly in the direction of a welfare state.

On issues of foreign policy, the Liberal Democrats have not infrequently been on the defensive in recent years. Their general formula has been "an independent foreign policy, within the framework of alliance with the West, particularly the United States." In this fashion, they have sought to encompass both the rising tide of Japanese nationalism and their own commitment to an American-Japanese alliance. On the one hand, they have stressed their desire for a "peaceful diplomacy" that harmonizes with domestic needs and is not the product of foreign pressure (this barb is aimed at Communist China, not the United States); their strong support for the United Nations Charter; and their hope for friendly relations with all nations, including the Soviet Union and Communist China, under the principle of noninterference with domestic affairs and mutual respect for each other's political and social systems. On the other hand, the conservatives have proclaimed themselves against neutralism and in firm alignment with the Western democracies.

They have also asserted that in order to ensure its security and peace, Japan should prepare the "minimum defense power needed to defend the country," first by supporting the security treaty with the United States until world peace has been stabilized, and, secondly, by providing its own defense power, "as an independent nation," against direct or indirect aggression.

The Socialist party in recent years has laid its heaviest stress upon foreign policy issues. It has assailed the conservative foreign policy as dangerous and subservient to the United States. The Socialists have called for a policy of "positive neutrality," aimed at establishing peace and the independence of Japan. They have urged close coöperation between Japan and the Asian-African states, so as to relax international tensions. And they have demanded the resumption of diplomatic relations between Japan and Communist China at the earliest possible date.

The Socialists also favor the complete neutralization of Japan. They have consistently opposed the security treaty with the United States, as is well known, and continue to demand its abolition, along with the removal of all American military bases from Japan. They support the gradual reduction of the Defense Force and its conversion into a National Land Development Force, with Japanese security being underwritten by the United Nations or through multilateral agreements. (We shall have more to say about the debate over alliance versus neutralism at a later point.)

On domestic economic issues, the Socialist party strikes out against various abuses: unemployment, low wages, and the general system of "monopoly capitalism," as they identify the Japanese economy. The Socialists argue for a "self-reliant" economy, long-range planning, controls over large industry, and emphasis upon consumer and worker benefits. Their aim is the ultimate establishment of a socialist economy.

The Democratic Socialist party made its unsuccessful debut in the 1960 election. Its foreign policy position was marked by an attack upon the Liberal Democrats for being subservient to the United States, and upon the Socialists for being subservient to the Soviet Union and Communist China. The Democratic Socialists called for a foreign policy independent of both the United States and the Soviet Union. They urged the "step-by-step abrogation" of the revised security treaty, the resumption of diplomatic relations with Communist China, and the normalization of relations with the Asian-African states—especially coöperation in economic development.

The Democratic Socialists also sought a middle ground on the issue of defense. They announced themselves as opposed both to the Liberal Democratic position of strengthening Japanese armament "in violation of the Constitution and public welfare," and to the Socialist position of total neutralization. The Democratic Socialist position was that reliance upon the United Nations for security was the best ultimate hope, but since this could not be realized at this time, the present defense force should be accepted "to the extent that it does not violate the Constitution or harm the public welfare."

On economic issues, the Democratic Socialists called for an eight-year plan that would double national income, expand trade, and modernize Japanese industry. They demanded an end to rising prices by tightening controls over industry and increased planning in production and distribution.

In terms of these various issues, as we suggested earlier, the conservatives would appear to have a considerable psychological and political advantage. There is ample evidence to suggest that the Japanese people are concerned about issues of war and peace, vaguely troubled over the question of their *raison d'être* in the modern world, and capable of being aroused by nationalist appeals. If these are issues more regularly felt in acute form by the elite, still they can under certain conditions produce major reverberations at the mass level. The conservatives are now well aware of this, but they are also aware of the fact that the most sustained and immediate issues for the ordinary Japanese citizen revolve around matters affecting livelihood. The Socialists stress foreign policy and ideology. At present, however, the average Japanese is only sporadically interested in foreign policy with sufficient intensity to support and sustain political action based on it. And he is not in an ideological mood. Indeed, in certain respects, he is not in a political mood. There is a difference, to be sure, between traditional and modern apathy. Traditional political apathy was and is the product of ignorance, grinding poverty, and the total acceptance of higher authority. These factors are still present in Japan in varying degree, but it is not they alone that produce apathy today. Modern political apathy springs from progress—from the intensive commitment of energies in directions other than politics, from achieving and wishing to enjoy new levels of material attainment. It is apathy in this form that has been emerging in Japan recently.

Thus the Socialist appeal to the "great issues," the cries for the masses to storm the barricades, face fundamental obstacles. Yet, in this matter as in many others, modern Japan represents a paradox. On the one hand, progress has produced its own form of political apathy at a time when traditional forms still exist. On the other hand, the inexorable, rapid movement toward modernity has automatically produced new potentialities for a mass movement when issues capable of triggering the explosion emerge.

The above considerations require that we give some attention to recent voting behavior in Japan. This will represent the last general check upon our earlier hypotheses prior to examining the May–June incidents of 1960 as a case study. Fortunately, the Election Bureau of the Local Autonomy Agency has conducted detailed surveys of recent elections. We shall concentrate upon the 1958 survey, with occasional references to earlier elections.[19] First, let us start with some broad indices of political consciousness and participation. On various occasions the Election Bureau has asked the question, "Have you ever seen or heard the words '*kōmei senkyo*' (fair election)?" The answers were as follows; in percentages:[20]

Answer	December, 1958	February, 1958	1953	1952
Yes	87	86	85	77
No	13	14	15	23

The "No" group did not vary significantly in its distribution between rural and urban districts. As might have been expected, women over sixty constituted about one half its numbers. Another general category strongly represented was those with low education.

Japan has always had a high voting rate. In the 1958 election, for example, 77 per cent of the registered voters cast ballots. Registration, moreover, is undertaken by the local election commissions, using all available records. Consequently, it is relatively complete, since it does not depend upon the initiative of the voter. It would be very dangerous, however, to equate this high voting rate with a high level of political consciousness and commitment. The following tabulation gives an urban-rural breakdown on non-voting, expressed in percentages:[21]

[19] The 1958 survey was entitled *Sōsenkyo no jittai* ("The Actual Conditions of the General Election") published in Tokyo by the Local Autonomy Board Election Bureau, December, 1958 (114 pp.).

[20] *Ibid.*, p. 9.

[21] This table is taken from Junichi Kyōgoku and Nobutaka Ike,

The Japanese Political Process

Non-Voting rates	1947	1949	1952	1953	1955	1958
Metropolitan areas	39	37	44	45	38	35
Urban (cities)	35	27	24	28	26	25
Semirural (towns)	31	19	18	21	21	19
Rural	33	21	17	19	17	16

It is to be noted that the highest voting rates are con-sistently in the rural and semirural areas. Does this mean that the farmer has a higher level of political consciousness than the resident of Tokyo or Osaka, where at least one third of the eligible voters do not vote? The answer must be sought in other directions. Every test indicates that the rural citizen is less well informed, and less politically conscious—as this concept is ordinarily employed—than the urbanite. In part, the higher voting rate is reflective of a higher degree of discipline and social pressure. Public authorities conduct a strenuous campaign to get out the vote. Often the theme is con-veyed that voting is a duty, not a right. Local bosses or leaders, moreover, exert every effort to get "their vote" out, and it is precisely in the areas where more traditional voting patterns are strong that the higher voting rates are recorded. These facts are also borne out by the following tabulation, which reveals that the voting rate reaches its highest level in local, rural elections:[22]

NATIONAL VOTING RATE IN VARIOUS ELECTIONS (In percentages)

Elections	1947	1949	1951	1952	1953	1955	1958	1959	1960
House of Representatives	68	74	. . .	76	74	76	77	. . .	70
Prefectural assemblies	82	. . .	83	. . .	. . .	77	. . .	79	. . .
Five largest city councils	?	. . .	62	. . .	. . .	62	. . .	65	. . .
Special district councils in Tokyo	73	. . .	75	. . .	. . .	62	. . .	65	. . .
City councils	?	. . .	90	. . .	. . .	85	. . .	86	. . .
Town and village councils	?	. . .	96	. . .	. . .	92	. . .	93	. . .

"Voting Behavior in Postwar General Elections," *Shisō,* August, 1960, p. 30.

[22] *Sōsenkyo no jittai,* pp. 16–17.

Also of importance is the question of how the voters react to the election process. Here, again, we have statistics based upon the 1958 election. Immediately following that election, the Election Board poll was conducted, and the voters sampled were asked, "Do you think this election was conducted fairly and correctly?" Fifty-nine per cent answered "Yes" and 19 per cent "No"; 22 per cent stated that they did not know. The highest percentage of "No" answers came from the younger and more highly educated groups. For example, 55 per cent of those with university and college education answered "Yes," while 38 per cent answered "No." The question was also asked, "Do you think that all the candidates in your district abided by the election laws, or were there many who violated these?" Twenty per cent replied that all candidates abided by the laws, 29 per cent asserted that some candidates violated the laws but the majority abided by them, 10 per cent answered that many candidates violated the laws, 1 per cent stated that all candidates violated the laws, and 40 per cent said that they did not know. Again, it was the younger, more educated males who indicated in largest numbers their belief that there had been some or many violations. On the other hand, an overwhelming number of voters indicated that they thought elections could be clean. The question was asked, "Are gifts of money and goods or the use of entertainment at election time things that cannot be avoided?" Five per cent said these things could not be avoided, but 82 per cent said they could be, and 13 per cent were undecided.

If accurate, these figures would indicate that the majority of Japanese citizens are either reasonably well satisfied with current elections or not greatly concerned. There is a minority, however, largely from the younger and more highly educated male category, that is dissatisfied. The indications are that there is a strong correlation between the upper levels of political consciousness and sophistication (as measured by education, definite positions on issues, and identification with party) and a higher rate of dissatisfaction—especially from that segment on the "left."

Most interesting were the questions that shed light upon the voters' methods and degree of preparation for casting their ballots. It might be noted again that under present regulations, each voter may cast one ballot for the office of representative in the lower house of the Diet, and he casts this ballot by writing in the name of the candidate. After the 1958 election, voters were asked a series of questions relating to the amount of information they possessed on the parties and candidates, and the sources of that information. First, those polled were asked, "Did you read or hear the programs of the Liberal Democratic and the Socialist parties?" Exactly one half of those responding stated that they had read or heard the Liberal Democratic party program; the other 50 per cent stated that they had not read or heard it. Forty-five per cent had read or heard the Socialist party program, whereas 55 per cent had not.

A series of questions followed that related to the contact of the voters with the major methods whereby the parties and candidates campaigned and sought to win support. We give the main questions and the responses, in percentages, below.[23] (The first column represents those replying who voted—85 per cent of the total respondents; the second column, with the figures in parentheses, includes those who did not vote.)

1. "Did you look at the official election brochure which contained the names, pictures, and political views of all the candidates? If so, did you read it? If you read it, did you read it all, parts of it, or just the section on the candidate for whom you voted?"

Response:

a) Read entire brochure	32 ⎤		(38) ⎤	
b) Did not read entire brochure, but did read more than the section on my candidate	25 ⎬ 63		(29) ⎬ (74)	
c) Read only the section on my candidate	6 ⎦		(7) ⎦	
d) Did not read brochure	8		(9)	
e) Did not see brochure	14		(17)	

2. "Did you listen to the candidates on the radio?"

Response:

a) Heard all candidates	14 ⎤		(16) ⎤	
b) Did not hear all, but heard more than my candidate	32 ⎬ 49		(37) ⎬ (57)	
c) Heard only my candidate	3 ⎦		(4) ⎦	

[23] *Ibid.*, pp. 25–39.

d) Heard others, but not my candidate	4	(5)
e) Did not hear or did not know about broadcasts	32	(38)

3. "Did you see the advertisements run in the newspapers on behalf of the candidates, and notices giving the times of their radio broadcasts?"

Response:

a) Saw all advertisements	16 ⎤		(18) ⎤	
b) Did not see all, but saw more than those of my candidate	29 ⎬ 49		(35) ⎬ (56)	
c) Saw only those of my candidate	4 ⎦		(4) ⎦	
d) Saw others, but not those of my candidate	4		(5)	
e) Did not see or know about any advertisements	32		(38)	

4. "Did you hear any street-corner speeches by candidates of your district? Did you hear your candidate?"

Response:

a) Heard my candidate	24	(28)
b) Did not hear my candidate, but heard others	8	(10)
c) Did not hear any such speeches	53	(62)

5. "Did you go to any candidate meetings in your district? If so, were they for an individual candidate or were they joint meetings?"

Response:

a) Individual candidate meeting	7	(8)
b) Joint candidates meeting	9	(10)
c) Both types	2	(3)
d) Did not go to any meetings	67	(79)

From the above responses, the Election Bureau constructed the following tabulation, in percentages, of the relative impact or effectiveness of the various forms of contact or mass media communication.[24] All respondents—including those who had not read, seen, or heard anything about any candidates—answered the question as to which media of information could be utilized by them to best advantage.

[24] *Ibid.,* p. 36.

The Japanese Political Process

Respondents	Election brochures	Radio political broadcasts	Newspaper advertise-ments	Street speeches	Independent and joint candidate meetings
Persons who saw, read about, or heard all candidates	71	53	53	32	18
Persons who saw, read about, or heard their own candidate	63	49	49	24	17
Persons who did not read about, see, or hear any candidate	14	32	32	53	67

(Presumably, the high percentages recorded in the last two columns for the third category of persons should be attributed to their poor reading and comprehension ability, and to their relative lack of contact with mass media.)

Another type of check was provided on the relative effectiveness of various types of campaigning or contact. The question was asked: "What stands out as the thing that made up your mind upon whom you would vote for?" [25] The responses were as follows (in percentages):

Election brochures	41
Joint candidate meetings	10
Independent candidate meetings	6
Street speeches	12
Newspaper advertisements	19
Radio broadcasts where candidate gave political views	24
Radio broadcasts where candidate gave personal background and experience	9
Postcard received	9
Other things	2
Nothing stands out	19
Total	145 (multiple answers were accepted)

[25] *Ibid.*, pp. 39–40.

The Japanese Political Process

On the basis of all the data given above, the Election Bureau set up a "Table of Political Consciousness Concerning This Election"[26] (see accompanying table).

According to the 1958 poll, 56 per cent of the voters did not talk with any member of their household concerning how they intended to vote, and 76 per cent of the voters did not discuss their vote with anyone outside the household. When asked whether their vote was influenced by any person or organization, the following replies were received:[27]

Reply	Percentage
Aid from knowledgeable person	8
Instruction from union or other association	3
Coöperative help from within the district or *buraku*	1
Aid from prominent person	2
Aid from official	1
No special influence	87
Total	102 (multiple answers were allowed)

If the statistics relating to voter methods and degree of preparation for casting ballots are reasonably accurate, a number of interesting facts are revealed. Clearly, the election brochure is the most widely used and effective method of presenting the candi-

[26] *Ibid.*, p. 44.

[27] *Ibid.*, p. 50. The Shimane Prefecture survey noted earlier indicated that between 25 and 30 per cent of the voters had been approached by "bosses" or neighborhood association leaders. On the other hand, a Tokyo 1952 survey suggested that less than 10 per cent of the voters (except union members) had been asked personally to support a candidate or belonged to associations that had decided to support a candidate. Of the union members, 24 per cent replied that they belonged to unions that had agreed to support a given candidate, and of this 24 per cent, 56 per cent stated that they had complied with the decision (Rōyama *et al., op. cit.,* p. 103). Another survey taken among workers indicated that 35 per cent believed newspapers, radio, and magazines to be the most influential in determining their votes; 27 per cent picked the recommendations or decisions of unions or workshops; and 9 per cent stated that suggestions of friends, relatives, or "bosses" (Fujiwara, *op. cit.,* Appendix, p. 116).

Those who knew concretely the political programs of both the Liberal Democratic Party and the Japan Socialist Party — Those who had read the brochure concerning their candidate . . . . A 19%

Those who knew concretely the difference between the Liberal Democratic Party and Japan Socialist Party programs . . . . . . — Those who had not read the brochure . . . . . . B 16%

Those who did not know the differences in the programs
- Those who had read the brochure concerning their candidate — Those who knew that candidate's political views and personal qualifications had appeared in newspaper ads
- Those who had not read the brochure — Those who did not know that candidate's political views and personal qualifications had appeared in newspaper ads

{ Those seeing newspaper ads for candidates other than their own . . . . . C 30%

Others. . . . . D 24%

E 11%

Table of Political Consciousness Concerning Election

date to the voters. Some three-fourths of the voters made use of the brochure. More than one half of them heard political radio broadcasts, and approximately the same number read political advertisements in the newspapers. When voters were asked what helped most in making up their minds on candidates, however, the radio broadcasts had a substantial edge over the newspaper advertisements. Other forms of candidate-voter contact had far less impact numerically. However, the group who voted for the candidate they heard at a meeting represent the real "activist" element among the electorate, and generally it was they who used the other media most fully. Typically, they were younger, more highly educated males from urban areas.

If we accept the Election Bureau "Table of Political Consciousness," roughly one fifth of the voters can be placed in the top category and considered "well informed" in terms of party platforms and candidate views. A total of one third of the voters can be placed in a category of "well informed or fairly well informed," taking Election Bureau categories *A* and *B*. Two thirds of the Japanese electorate, however, must be classified as poorly informed or not informed at all, if Election Bureau figures are accepted. Still, a very small percentage of voters admitted seeking or receiving outside assistance in connection with their voting decision. Eighty-seven per cent asserted that there was no particular influence or external advice which effected their vote. This figure is very doubtful. Influence or "assistance" may be so routine or so subtle as not to be recognized; moreover, there is undoubtedly a reluctance to admit such influence at present.

The most critical survey materials, of course, pertain to the vote itself. The 1958 survey did not produce a vote[28] identical

Party	Survey	Actual election results
Liberal Democratic	66	58
Japan Socialist	29	33
Japan Communist	1	2
Minor Parties	0	1
Independents	2	6
Don't know	2	. . .

[28] *Ibid.*, pp. 53–59.

with the actual elections results, as the preceding figures will indicate.

It is thought that some respondents identified the independent candidates with the Liberal Democratic party in the survey, but the poll was still somewhat weighted in favor of the conservatives. Nevertheless, the distribution of the vote as shown in Chart 16 undoubtedly gives an accurate indication of the basic factors that governed this and other recent Japanese elections. What are the most significant points to be emphasized? First, while the conservatives carried all areas handily, their margins became progressively heavier as they went from metropolitan to rural areas. In the six metropolitan centers, the survey gave the Liberal Democratic party 41 per cent and the Japan Socialist party 30 per cent, but in the most rural areas the votes were 63 and 23 per cent, respectively. The continuing hold possessed by the conservatives in the rural sectors of Japanese society is once again clearly revealed.

The survey indicates no substantial difference in party preference between men and women voters. The age factor, however, did produce important differences. The Liberal Democrats barely carried the twenty- to twenty-four-year-old group, especially the males. Conservative strength relative to that of the Socialists steadily increased with each age category, reaching a 72–10 ratio with males sixty years of age and older. Does this fact give the Socialists great hope for the future, or is socialism primarily a proclivity of youth? The practical answer to this question will be spelled out in terms of concrete conditions and trends, and the alternative programs available. The conservatives are well aware of this fact when they advance their own welfare policies. Their future depends upon their capacity to move with the times.

The socioeconomic complexion of the 1958 vote sustains many of our earlier themes. The conservatives scored heavily with agrarian and commercial-industrial elements, whereas the socialists polled a majority of votes from the technical, white-collar, and laboring classes. It is interesting to note that the Socialist plurality was actually higher within the first two groups, and weaker within labor. This is also supported by the evidence obtained when the vote is divided on the basis of rough economic classifications.

The Socialists did best within the lower-middle-class and middle-class categories. The lower-class economic category—the weakest agrarian and laboring element in Japanese society—is in general unorganized, traditionalist in outlook, and conservative in dominant voting pattern, with a high rate of absenteeism. To a considerable extent, a distribution of the vote within educational categories buttresses these conclusions. The Socialist vote was highest within the most highly educated group, the postwar university and prewar higher and technical school graduates. This reflects Socialist strength among the intellectuals, and penetration into the Japanese middle class. Indeed, the Socialist proportion of the vote dropped steadily with a decrease in education, declining in the primary school category to 15 per cent, as opposed to 58 per cent for the Liberal Democrats and 23 per cent not voting. The real "proletariat" vote is strongly conservative. The upwardly mobile elements within Japanese society, especially the lower middle class—organized labor, white-collar employees, and technicians—tend to vote Socialist in greatest proportion, along with an important segment of the intellectuals.

The reasons given for their vote by those polled are of equal interest and importance to the vote itself.[29] Chart 17 sets forth sixteen specific reasons on which a count was taken. These reasons can be divided into three basic categories. The first category relates to the character or personality of the candidate and the personal ties between him and the voter. The reasons fitting this category are those with the letters *A* (liked his character), *H* (because everyone said good things about him), *I* (because I knew him well), *O* (because candidate is related to me), and *P* (because I am indebted to candidate). A second category reflects party loyalty and decisions based upon reading about, hearing, or seeing some part of the campaign. The reasons fitting this category are those with the letters *B* (support the party), *C* (saw the brochure), *D* (heard radio speech), *G* (heard public speech), *E* (saw newspaper advertisement), and probably *M* (message from candidate). Finally, a third category relates essentially to impersonal decisions motivated

[29] *Ibid.,* pp. 59–76.

in some degree by an external source or sources. The reasons fitting this category are those with the letters F (household conference), J (request from knowledgeable person), L (advice from knowledgeable person), K (advice from union or association), and N (decision of town or hamlet).

The 1958 survey indicates that the second category of reasons was the most important one, with the first category in second place, and the third category trailing far behind. When multiple answers were tallied, those who actually voted registered 103, 53, and 21 per cent, respectively, for these categories; when only the principal answer was recorded, the respective figures were 36, 30, and 9 per cent. (In both cases, these percentage figures are based on 85 per cent of the total sample—that is, the number of actual voters polled.) One may question the reliability of these figures. In particular, the figures for the third category seem suspiciously low. There is no reason, however, not to accept the poll as generally indicative of the relative position of various motivations and stimuli involved in Japanese voting behavior.

Chart 18 contains a detailed breakdown of the incidence of these three categories, divided by area, sex, age, occupation, education, economic position, scale of political consciousness, and party. Not all of the figures here are strongly meaningful, since one is dealing with a number of cross variables. For example, two types of individuals susceptible to the motivations and stimuli of the second category are the highly educated, well-to-do, urban male businessman who is a conservative and the urban male laborer of lower middle class and modest education who is a trade unionist and socialist. Nevertheless, we can say that the second category, being in some degree reflective of "modern," "rational," and "sophisticated" political behavior, is generally strongest in the areas and with the people associated with such qualities. Typically, this means younger males, residing in metropolitan centers, whose occupations may range from the technical, white-collar, or labor fields to those of commerce and industry. When the measurement is based upon education or economic group, statistical probability favors the higher-placed groups, and this is quite pronounced when the Election Bureau scale of political consciousness is applied,

The Japanese Political Process

Category *A* (highest consciousness) having a decided margin in favor of the second category, as one would expect. Division by party, however, strongly favors the Socialists, indicative in part of their urban orientation and the higher degree of party loyalty and discipline they have sought to inculcate in their followers. Here again, however, the figures might be misleading, because it is not easy to separate the factors involved in the entrenched conservative voting pattern of the rural areas.

The first category, which we might designate as the "personal preference" category, is clearly of high importance to Japanese voters. The citizen most prone to be influenced by the reasons fitting into this category is typically a middle-aged or older rural female, relatively low in education, economic status, and political consciousness, who votes for the conservative party. The third category, which we might call "ratification of authority" has a much more pronounced correlation with the highest end of the age scale, and the lowest end of the education, economic class, and political consciousness scales. In short, it follows the pattern of the first category, but in much more extreme form.

When those polled were asked specifically to which factor they gave the most weight, the party or the character of the candidate, the following percentage distribution was obtained (with percentages of the non-voters included in parentheses):[30]

Party	28	(32)
Candidate	38	(45)
Both—Can't say	8	(10)
Don't know	11	(13)
Total	85	(100)

By party, this answer was divided as follows:

	Party	Candidate	Both—Can't say	Don't know
Liberal Democratic party	27	49	10	14
Japan Socialist party	46	35	9	10
Japan Communist party	54	33	...	13

[30] *Ibid.,* p. 65.

Nine press polls on party-candidate preference reveal similar divisions:

Year	Press	Party	Candidate	Both	Other or Don't Know
1952	Asahi	25	43	17	15
1953	Asahi	39	46	5	10
1953	Asahi	35	50	7	8
1954	Press Federation	21	41	16	22
1955	Asahi	27	45	13	15
1955	Press Federation	35	40	?	?
1958	Jiji	25	36	16	23
1958	Mainichi	35	44	. .	21
1958	Yomiuri	29	38	27	6

These figures would indicate that a decisive majority of the conservative voters in Japan weigh the character of the candidate more heavily than the question of party affiliation, whereas the reverse position is taken by the Socialist and Communist voters. In general terms, this is probably accurate. Once again, however, one must be extremely cautious in relying too heavily upon such statistics. On the one hand, to draw a line between party and candidate orientation among those voters who invariably vote for the candidate of one party is not easy, even if we can assert with some confidence that the basic stimuli appear to be personal ones. And, on the other hand, the Election Bureau discovered in the 1958 survey that 36 per cent of those who stated that they valued party over candidate had actually voted for a candidate of another party in the 1955 election. Perhaps this general point can be summarized as follows: the evidence available would indicate that no more than one third (probably less) of the Japanese voters at present are consciously committed to voting on the basis of party affiliation.

Using the voting statistics presented above and other data introduced earlier, we can set forth three broad categories or types of Japanese voting behavior that exist at this time, categories that parallel those noted in connection with the answers given by respondents in the 1958 survey to the question of what factors determined their vote. The most traditional form of voting be-

The Japanese Political Process

havior in Japan is the ratification of authority. In such cases, the voter does not choose a candidate on the basis of party or even personal preference. Voting is rather an impersonal action connected with group behavior and the ratification of authority in their traditional Japanese forms.

The most deeply rooted, historic form of Japanese social organization has been the small, relatively exclusive mutual-help group. In such units, individual interests or choices are subordinated to the demands or consensus of the group. There is, however, a recognized division between leadership and simple membership roles in the group. Leaders extend their benevolence, that is, they take care of the group interests, and members reciprocate by accepting the authority of the leader or "boss." As noted much earlier, this is the social basis for the political faction. In terms of voting, it means essentially subordinating one's personal choice for the choice designated by the leader.

This pattern of social organization and political behavior derived from the culture of an intensive agrarian, familial society. It stemmed from the historic relationship commonly existing between landlord or wealthy farmer and tenant or poor farmer, or, at a different level, between samurai (warrior) and daimyo (feudal lord). It was nurtured and sustained by a highly developed value system drawn from the familial and kinship models of this socioeconomic system. It has been projected into the modern era with varying modifications. Traditional behavior in all its forms still has far-reaching political significance for contemporary Japan. In purely electoral terms, it represents the ability or potential of a boss to deliver a bloc vote once he has arranged a consensus within his group. The position of the boss, indeed, may help to explain various interesting factors about the rural vote in particular.[31] For

[31] For some excellent pioneer studies in English on political differences and trends in urban and rural Japan, see Kyōgoku and Ike, *Urban-Rural Differences in Voting Behavior in Postwar Japan,* previously cited, Robert E. Ward, "Urban-Rural Differences and the Process of Political Modernization in Japan: A Case Study," *Economic Development and Cultural Change,* IX, No. 1, Part II (October, 1960), pp. 135–165; and Robert Ward's section in *Village Japan* previously cited.

example, voters accepting the position of a leader or a group account in part for the simultaneous existence in rural areas of a high voting rate and a high indifference-ignorance rate with respect to candidates and issues.

It would be erroneous to limit traditional behavior to rural groups alone. In various degrees, such behavior is prevalent in all groups, at all levels of Japanese society. The polls are very likely to miss the full potency of this factor, because it is habitualized behavior, often related more to the subconscious than to the conscious, and, therefore, not easily elicited in questioning. But the politicians are well aware of its importance. A candidate's organization typically consists of a loose network of "bosses," including mayors, prefectural assemblymen, and local council members. These men, as we have noted, serve as the vote mobilizers for a Diet candidate by virtue of their personal influence and the respect locally accorded them. Thus the relation between the voter and the national candidate is often an indirect one, via a prominent local personage.

There can be little doubt, however, that the trend is away from "traditional" and toward "modern" voting behavior, as the polls have detected. Local bosses are less and less able to predict or deliver the vote. A study carried out in Okayama Prefecture in 1956 indicated a substantial difference between prewar and postwar patterns of geographic support for candidates.[32] Before the war, a candidate's support was usually concentrated. It came from a few pockets or "campaign bases" within his district. Since 1945, however, the pattern of support has become more diffuse, being spread more evenly throughout the constituency and not coming merely from a few isolated sectors. As was briefly noted earlier, this suggests that the traditional *jiban* structure, with its premium upon local bosses who can deliver the votes of their entire group, is declining in importance, and the candidate's dependence upon the support of independent constituents is becoming much heavier. Even to the extent that leadership is important, significant changes are taking place. A new type of local leader like the Agricultural Coöperative leader is emerging in many villages and towns. His in-

[32] Beardsley, Hall, and Ward, *op. cit.*, pp. 422–441.

fluence comes mainly from his ability to manage the local economy and negotiate effectively with prefectural and national government, or urban business interests, rather than from factors of traditional prestige and family ties. Such trends, of course, are related to the whole modernization process that has engulfed Japanese society.

There are, however, at least two basic types or categories of individual voting behavior. One is governed by personal, emotional, and value-implying reactions that center around the character and personality of the candidate. This type of behavior is "candidate-oriented" in a very special sense. The second basic type of individual voting behavior is governed by an impersonal evaluation of "what the candidate can do for me," emphasizing such factors as his party affiliation, his connections with interest groups, and his promises, gifts, and favors. We have earlier called this type of voting behavior "modern," "rational," and "sophisticated." We have set it at the opposite end of the continuum from "traditional" behavior. These terms can certainly be defended, but they also reflect a modern, urban, industrial perspective and bias. We are likely to underestimate the degree of political sophistication possessed by the "traditional" peasant *for the purposes of his environment,* and the extent to which he kept in mind his own self-interest and that of his immediate family. It is also imperative, of course, to understand that rarely if ever does one of these categories of political behavior operate in its pure form. Especially in the modern period, we are concerned with complex mixtures.

Nevertheless, all signs point to a trend away from forms of voting behavior that represent mere ratification of authority and toward forms that represent individual decision making. Within the framework of individual decision making, increasing emphasis is being given to criteria that represent the voter's evaluation of his self-interest, rather than to judgments of the candidates' personality and character. There is still a pronounced difference in this respect, as in others, between urban and rural communities. That difference is probably narrowing, however, and everywhere the "modernization" quotient in Japanese politics is rising.

THE CRISIS OF

MAY–JUNE, 1960

—A CASE STUDY

As we noted at the outset of this study, Japan has recently experienced the greatest mass movement in her political history. Millions of Japanese participated directly in the political events of May and June, 1960.[1] They signed petitions, engaged in work stoppages, demonstrated in Tokyo streets, or took similar actions. Almost all of these actions, it will be noted, took place outside the framework of the party movement and the Diet or on their peripheries. In some respects, the parties never seemed weaker than in this period of troubles—*all* the parties.

[1] For a variety of views on the May–June incidents, in English, see "Japanese Intellectuals Discuss American-Japanese Relations," Introduction by Robert A. Scalapino and articles by Kanichi Fukuda, Makoto Saitō, Yoshikazu Sakamoto, and Takeshi Ishida, *Far Eastern Survey*, October, 1960, pp. 145–160; "Japan Today," Introduction by I. I. Morris and articles by Kiyoshi Nasu, Kōsaku Tamura, Kikuo Nakamura, Kazuo Kuroda, and Sadachika Nabeyama, supplement to *The New Leader*, November 28, 1960, 42 pp.; Edwin O. Reischauer, "The Broken Dialogue with Japan," *Foreign Affairs*, XXXIX, No. 1 (October, 1960), 11–26; David Wurfel, "The Violent and the Voiceless in Japanese Politics," *Contemporary Japan*, XXXVI, No. 4 (November, 1960), 663–694; "To Our Friends in America," a pamphlet containing statements by Hisaakira Kano, Takashi Komatsu, Shigeo Horie, Masatoshi Matsushita, and Seiichi Fukuoka (published by Radio Japan, n.d.).

The Crisis of May-June, 1960

The immediate issue at stake was the revised United States–Japan Security Treaty. Negotiations between the two countries over treaty revision had been long and arduous. From the standpoint of American authorities, significant concessions had been made. These related to such subjects as the disposition and use of American forces stationed in Japan. None of the concessions, however, removed the fundamental objections of the neutralists, who saw the revised treaty as a "legalization" of a condition previously imposed upon a subjugated state. The original treaty could not be defended as a product of negotiations between equals, and this fact, together with its substantive inequities, made it more vulnerable, hence potentially more temporary. To remove some or all of the inequities, and to do this in the course of negotiations when Japan was fully sovereign, was to project the American-Japanese military alliance at least a full decade into the future. Since the neutralist objection was to the alliance itself, its improvement could scarcely satisfy them.

As we noted earlier, the merits of alliance versus neutralism have been hotly debated in Japan for more than a decade. The policy of alliance with the United States has had strong support, despite the attacks leveled upon it. Its adherents have insisted that the American-Japanese alliance serves the causes of peace and prosperity. Their views, in composite form, can be set forth as follows:

a) Surrounded by formidable and hostile powers, Japan cannot risk neutralism. The Communist world does not recognize neutralism as legitimate. Hence, any agreement reached between Japan and the Communists on this basis would be violated or abrogated unilaterally by them if it suited their purposes. Experience thus far has indicated that neither the Soviet Union nor Communist China is willing to make any significant concessions to Japanese national interests. For Japan to be isolated, defenseless, or wholly dependent upon some vague international agreement would be more dangerous to its peace and security than military alliance with the United States.

b) At this juncture of world history, major war between the Communist and non-Communist forces is most likely to be avoided if a global balance of power can be maintained, it is argued. Japan has a moral responsibility to assist in the maintenance of that balance within the limits imposed upon her by constitutional provisions and internal economic-political conditions. These limitations preclude any rapid or extensive rearmament. They make impossible the use of Japanese forces overseas. They also make inadvisable the development of any nuclear weapons, or, indeed, the storing of such weapons in Japan for possible American use. But Japan can and should assist in maintaining non-Communist strength in Asia by allowing the United States to use air and naval facilities in exchange for an American guarantee to underwrite Japanese security.

     c) It is also argued that what is moral happily coincides with what is politically and economically advantageous. It is proper for Japan, now en route to democracy, to align itself with a nation having similar political values and institutions. And, on balance, this alliance has fostered rather than precluded the rapid establishment of a vast network of world contacts. To have had the United States as ally and supporter has greatly facilitated the reëntrance of Japan into the world scene. She has been able to participate in international and regional organizations much earlier than would otherwise have been possible, and to assume an active, important role in world affairs. The alliance has not hindered the development of ties with the non-aligned world; on the contrary, in certain respects, especially through its economic benefits, it has aided such contacts. Despite the alliance, normal relations have been reëstablished with the Soviet Union. More than this, Japan has never been able to attain. Admittedly, the alliance has adversely affected relations with Communist China. This is unfortunate, and efforts must be made to obtain improvements. But this problem does not offset the sizable political advantages gained by Japan as a result of her alliance with the United States.

     d) The most important advantage, however, has been an economic one. The American alliance, according to its proponents, must be given credit for being a major factor in the unprecedented prosperity which Japan has enjoyed during the past decade. First, by means of extensive gifts, loans, and technical aid, the United States launched Japan on the road to economic recovery and growth. All forms of assistance, including military procurement, represented billions of dollars put into the Japanese economy. There was no alternative to this support, and without it the Japanese people would have faced unending misery and crisis. But money cannot measure the worth of the most basic economic assistance, namely, the transferral of vast quantities of technical, scientific, and managerial knowledge pertaining to the whole field of economic modernization. The tremendous technological revolution now taking place in Japan can be attributed in considerable measure to the far-reaching alliance with the United States, private and public. Thousands of Japanese have had advanced training in the United States; large numbers of American technicians and counselors have taught, advised, and learned in Japan. Patent sharing and many other forms of industrial coöperation have expanded greatly in recent years. The United States and Japan are partners in a revolution that is transforming the life of every Japanese citizen.

e) Closely connected with these developments has been the great surge in trade between the two societies. In 1960, Japan exported over one billion, one hundred million dollars' worth of goods to the United States, while her imports from that country totaled more than one billion, three hundred million dollars. Approximately one third of all Japanese trade was with the United States and Canada. The United States took 28 per cent of all Japanese exports, and furnished 30 per cent of all imports. The economic future of Japan hinges upon the maintenance and, if possible, the expansion of these relations. Any shift to a neutralist foreign policy would surely jeopardize the present economic ties with the United States, and thereby affect adversely every individual in Japan.

Thus do the supporters of alliance outline and defend their case. And to meet socialist challenges of subservience, the conservative leaders have proclaimed their objective as that of "an independent foreign policy within the framework of coöperation with the West, particularly the United States." They have asserted that they are seeking partnership, not subordination. They have insisted that their firm position during the negotiations for a revised security treaty resulted in the elimination of inequities. (The conservatives did bargain in a tough fashion with American authorities on some issues.) The conservatives have also repeatedly asserted that the alliance does not preclude an independent foreign policy, including some positions differing from the policy of the United States.

Indeed, the conservatives have carried the fight over Japanese independence to the socialists. They have insisted that if Japan is to be truly independent, it must have the power to defend itself. Consequently, they have urged the repeal of the so-called antiwar clause, Article Nine of the constitution. And in answer to the objections of the Soviet Union and Communist China, Japanese leaders have argued that their military alliance with the United States is for defensive purposes only, citing the fact that their forces total only 230,000 men at present, together with some 50,000 Americans in the area, a small group in comparison to the nearly three million men in the Chinese Communist armed force.

The policy of military alliance with the United States probably has positive support from about one third of the Japanese people, with an additional third being uncertain or indifferent. However, polls on certain issues or at certain times would appreciably raise or lower that number. For example, it appears that a considerable number of Japanese now support limited rearmament for defense purposes only. It is the issue of American bases in Japan and, thus, the direct connection with American military strategy pertaining to Asia, that seems to raise the most serious doubts. While the military aspects of the American-Japanese alliance remain vulnerable, a certain counterbalance is provided by the high degree of support given the economic and cultural aspects of the alliance.

Despite the various arguments advanced for the alliance, however, public opinion polls would indicate that neutralism has had a positive appeal to at least one third of the Japanese people.[2] Many of the reasons are obvious. The disaster of World

[2] In each edition, the *Asahi nenkan* ("Asahi Yearbook") gives a full account of the polls and survey research undertaken by the newspapers

War II has not been forgotten, nor will it be forgotten soon—230,000 Japanese still suffer from radioactive diseases as a result of the Hiroshima and Nagasaki bombings, and many thousands of other victims of the fire raids or of combat injuries serve as living reminders that the last war did not pay. There is an acute awareness of the vulnerability of Japan in this age of nuclear war. Her densely packed cities are now only minutes away from Soviet or Chinese bases. Her population, approaching 93,000,000 at present, lives in an area approximately the size of California. Foreign trade is indispensable to survival. Japan must import 80 per cent of her industrial raw materials and 20 per cent of her foodstuffs. The difficulties of supply in the event of war seem enormous. There is

Asahi Shimbun, Mainichi Shimbun, and *Yomiuri Shimbun,* and by other organizations.

In English, Douglas Mendel, Jr. presents and analyzes an important collection of poll data pertaining to foreign policy issues in his forthcoming book, *The Japanese People and Foreign Policy* (Berkeley and Los Angeles, 1962).

Two sets of polls on rearmament, one from the earlier period and one from a somewhat later time are as follows:

"Asahi Shimbun" Polls—1952–1954

(Percentage distribution)

Response	Feb., 1952	Feb., 1953	June, 1953	May, 1954
Rearmament Necessary	32	38	41	37
Rearmament Unnecessary	26	29	23	30
Under Certain Conditions	24	14	16	15
No Opinion	18	19	20	18

Source: *Asahi nenkan,* 1954, p. 306, and *Jiji nenkan* ("Current Events Yearbook"), 1955, p. 302.

Poll Conducted by the Prime Minister Secretariat

(Percentage distribution)

Response	Oct., 1956	Feb., 1957
For Rearmament	33	28
Against Rearmament	42	41
Under Certain Conditions	13	17
Don't Know	12	14

Source: *Asahi nenkan,* 1958, p. 259.

the additional problem of trade expansion in time of peace, with the argument that neutralism would open new markets without losing old ones.

We remarked earlier that neutralism is also an expression of nationalism in foreign policy. After an era of intensive occupation, perhaps the remarkable thing is that personal relations between Japanese and Americans have remained generally good. The United States has done well in "popularity" polls, and personal anti-Americanism has not shown any appreciable increase despite the rising nationalist sentiment and the dissatisfaction with certain American policies.[3] Sharper reactions might have been expected, given the historic Japanese tradition of isolation, xenophobia, and extreme national and individual sensitivity. In spite of the relatively moderate reaction to the Occupation era, however, the demand for "full independence" has been a strong one. In politics, the socialists have kept up a drumfire attack upon conservative foreign policy as subservient to the United States. They have denounced foreign bases not merely as dangerous, but also as symbols of the fact that the Occupation has not been completely liquidated. They have insisted that only through a neutralist policy can Japan assert her independence and her proper identity as an Asian state.

For many Japanese socialists, neutralism, in addition to its other virtues, is also an article of political faith. Pacifism and Marxism have both had a deep influence on the Japanese socialist movement. Each of these now lends its weight to the neutralist

[3] For example, in response to a Newspaper Public Opinion Survey League national poll in December, 1954, asking the question "Which country do you like?" 33.3 per cent answered, "the United States"; 26.3, "Great Britain"; 22.5, "Switzerland"; 22.3, "France"; and 11.9, "Communist China." "What country do you dislike?" got the following answers: 37.3 per cent answered, "the Soviet Union"; 30.3, "Korea"; 21.3, "Communist China"; and 10.6, "United States." (*Ibid.,* 1956, p. 320.)

Another national poll on the same subject, in November, 1957, produced the following results: "Which country do you like?"—26.5 per cent, "the United States," and 5.6, "India"; "Which country do you dislike?"—30.5 per cent, "the Soviet Union"; 4.0, "the United States"; and 3.7, "Communist China." (*Ibid.,* 1959, p. 158.)

cause. This may seem strange as applied to Marxism. It is true that Marxist-oriented Japanese socialists may *sound* as if they belonged to the Soviet camp. It is also true that some of them act that way. The combination of having the United States as the immediate, close-at-hand object of attack and of being trained only in Marxist terminology and methods of attack is conducive to a conscious or unconscious Communist bias.

But there is another important side to this picture. It is connected with the intricate history of Japanese socialism. The great majority of Marxists and quasi-Marxists within the Japanese socialist movement long ago broke away from the discipline of Moscow. Subsequently, the recriminations have often been bitter on both sides. Thus the postwar Japanese Socialist party, while increasingly dominated by its left wing, has not sought a broad popular front with the Communists. At home, as abroad, it has opted for neutralism. The majority of socialists continue to maintain a relatively orthodox Marxist position on many economic and political issues. This separates them decisively from the West, especially the United States. But their own experiences as well as their political instincts have caused them to seek identification with Nehru and the other Afro-Asian neutralists rather than with Khrushchev. Mao, as an Asian and a Chinese, has had somewhat more personal and political appeal, it must be admitted, but it is the traditional Nehru line that has constituted the basic socialist approach to world politics.

Against the background of the above debate and a rather evenly divided public opinion, the treaty crisis emerged. Initially, the anti-treaty movement was largely confined to the "professionals." Sōhyō attempted a national campaign, but this attracted little attention. Meanwhile, the socialists fought the treaty in the House of Representatives, using such tactics of questioning and delaying as were available to them. Prime Minister Kishi had visited Washington and signed the revised treaty on January 24, 1960. On February 4, it had been introduced into the lower house, with a special committee established to examine it. Naturally, the socialist minority sought to use the maximum time in debate. Between February 4 and May 19, when the treaty was forced to a vote, over a hundred days elapsed. Still, the opposition claimed that major sections of the treaty remained unclarified.

Notwithstanding the rather restricted and conventional opposition to the revised treaty prior to May 19, the foundations for a larger movement did exist, provided that some means were found to utilize these. We have noted many indications that the Japanese public has long been deeply disturbed about issues of armament and military alliance. While a majority may now accept the fact that Japan should have some type of military force for self-defense purposes, opposition to the revision of Article Nine, the antiwar clause of the new constitution, would seem to be substantial. Moreover, despite the general popularity of the United States noted earlier, the one *major* deficiency in the American image in Japan relates to issues of war and peace. More than any American "ally," the Japanese feel that the United States is making a limited contribution to peace; America is seen as being relatively military-minded.

This sentiment among the Japanese public has not been hidden from the Japanese conservatives, any more than from the socialists. It has made the former reluctant to speed up the tempo of rearmament, push for revision of Article Nine, or make any move in the direction of a regional defense pact. To add to conservative problems, on May 2 an American U-2 airplane was shot down over the territory of the Soviet Union. This had almost instant repercussions in Japan. The socialists charged that other American U-2 airplanes were based in Japan, and that these had been used for reconnaissance missions over Communist China, North Korea, and the Soviet Union. Both the Japanese government and the United States denied that any U-2 airplanes based in Japan had been used for espionage purposes. Nevertheless, public apprehension mounted. The subsequent collapse of the summit conference and the withdrawal of Khrushchev's invitation to President Eisenhower to visit Moscow also had a drastic effect upon the Japanese political scene. The revised treaty was now being debated in the context of a more strained world situation. The cold war was being intensified, and the risk of a hot war seemed much greater than in the recent past. Moreover, the symbolic significance of

The Crisis of May-June, 1960

Eisenhower's imminent visit to Japan had been drastically altered. Instead of coming as a representative of reduced tensions, major power accord, and coexistence—coming via Moscow—he was now scheduled to come via the Philippines, Taiwan, and Okinawa, as an inspector of American military bases in Asia. Naturally, this shift exacerbated the conservative-socialist cleavage in foreign policy, and greatly intensified the political strain upon Japanese society at large.

The Kishi government had long been in difficulties because of internal factionalism. Kishi perhaps represented the "compromise" type of leader, chosen less for his strength than for his capacity to adjust, a "neutral" in the midst of contending strong men. As we have noted, Kishi's position initially rested upon a five-faction coalition, the Kishi, Satō, Ishii, Ōno, and Kōno factions; subsequently, the Kōno faction dropped out of the coalition, and the Ikeda faction was substituted. The anti–Main Current factions within the Liberal Democratic party had been mounting a formidable campaign against the Kishi cabinet in the 1959–60 period. According to the reckoning of his conservative opponents, Kishi had been in power for a sufficient period; it was time to release the office of the prime-ministership to those who had waited so long— and so impatiently. Even the Main Current faction leaders had been watching for the chance to replace Kishi. He had also accumulated a number of enemies as a result of policy actions and inactions. His socialist opponents had always emphasized Kishi's membership in the Tōjō cabinet and his active role in the militarist era. The struggle over proposed revisions in the police and security laws had evoked cries of high-pressure tactics and a resurgence of reaction.[4] Thus, in terms both of its tenure and its tactics—along with some of its policies—the Kishi administration was close to a low ebb in the spring of 1960, with opponents inside and out of the party ready to put an end to it.

Because of the above factors, it was possible to unite professional agitators with a certain portion of both the Japanese elite and the urban masses in the events of late May and early

[4] See Masumi Junnosuke, "The Problem of the Police Duties Bill and Japanese Democracy," *Shisō*, February, 1959, pp. 1–19.

June, 1960. The catalytic force lay in the happenings of May 19. It was on this date that the Kishi government made its major drive for treaty ratification in the House of Representatives. The date was not an accident. If the revised treaty were approved by the lower house on May 19, it could come into effect one month later, at the time of the Eisenhower visit. (Under Japanese constitutional provisions, a treaty comes into effect automatically thirty days after ratification by the House of Representatives, if not approved before that time by the House of Councilors.)

It is easy to understand why an administration not overly popular at the moment, and hard pressed by its opponents on a dangerous issue, would seize upon the Eisenhower visit as an excellent political opportunity and seek to connect treaty ratification with that visit. It is equally easy to understand why all Kishi opponents, including those within the Liberal Democratic party, would seek to thwart that strategy. Thus the Kishi cabinet in developing its plans faced bitter opposition both from the anti–Main Current factions of its party and from the socialists. Because of the opposition within the Liberal Democratic party itself, the Kishi government felt compelled to cloak its strategy even from some of the members of its own party. Thus the decision to push through a motion to extend the Diet session and a second motion to approve the revised treaty on the evening of May 19 were not known to many conservatives in advance. This was, in fact, not a strategy of the Liberal Democratic party, but of the Main Current faction of that party.

Moreover, it was a strategy that had to be mounted against increasing chaos and violence within the Diet. With a portion of the Liberal Democrats looking on as passive bystanders, the socialists mounted the ramparts and, in a very literal sense, defied the government to pass. To stop passage of a Steering Committee resolution prolonging the Diet session, socialist members of the lower house sought to prevent the May 19 session from being opened by engaging in a "sit-down" movement. To keep the Speaker from reaching the rostrum, the socialists placed themselves on the floor, between the Speaker's Chamber and the front of the house. The government then ordered some five hundred police to drag the socialists off the floor. The plenary session thus opened with only conservatives taking part.

Parliamentary procedures on this day completely broke down. Along with the melee on the floor of the house, chaos reigned in a meeting of the Special Committee on the Security Treaty which was being held at approximately the same time. The socialists sought to put a vote of nonconfidence (which takes precedence over other bills), but the chairman refused to recognize the movers and later announced that the revised security treaty and related agreements had been passed by a majority of the committee. The entire meeting lasted only a few minutes and was marked by such complete confusion and shouting that no one could be certain of the actions taken.

Against this background, and with all socialists and some conservatives absent, during the midnight period of May 19–20 the Kishi elements within the Liberal Democratic party proceeded to vote an extension of the session beyond midnight and then to pass the revised treaty. These actions were accomplished with great speed, and with some anti-Kishi conservatives later claiming that they had not been informed of the actions which were to take place.[5]

This "May 19 incident" was violently attacked by almost all of the leading Japanese newspapers. While there was some criticism of the socialist obstructionist tactics, the attack was largely concentrated upon the "anti-democratic" actions of the Kishi cabinet. The "movement to defend democracy" had its origins in this event. And suddenly many elements hitherto passive joined in the anti-Kishi movement. This gave the movement qualities of spontaneity, diversity, and enthusiasm which it had previously lacked. It is impossible to understand post–May 19 developments without realizing that numerous currents were flowing with few connecting channels. The professional agitators were still very much in the

[5] For critical views of the famous midnight session see Ukai Nobushige, "Points at Issue in the Highhanded Adoption," *Shisō*, pp. 126–128, and Hashimoto Kiminobu, "It Is Legally Invalid Too," *Chūō Kōron*, July, 1960, pp. 42–46; also see the articles by Fukuda, Saitō, Sakamoto, and Ishida in *Far Eastern Survey*, October, 1960 (note 1).

scene, occupying critical leadership positions in some areas. Now, however, they had a rank-and-file following which their own actions alone could not possibly have produced. In the all-important student arena, leaders of Zengakuren—the national student federation— exercised key leadership roles. Zengakuren has long occupied an extreme-left political position; like many organizations, its official position and that of its leaders is far more radical than the political stance of the great bulk of its rank-and-file membership.

The Japanese political situation after May 19, however, provided Zengakuren leaders with an excellent opportunity to mobilize a truly mass movement on behalf of specific objectives, those of causing the Kishi government to resign and paving the way for new elections, with the revised treaty being made the central issue before the Japanese electorate. For the first time in its history, Zengakuren had a series of issues with much broader appeal than its own set of Marxist doctrines could possibly provide. But it also faced a major handicap, namely, the ideological divisions within its top ranks. Like all other elements of the Japanese left, Zengakuren has been rent by serious ideological cleavages. In a curious reflection of postwar Japanese freedom, one portion of the student far left has seized upon such events as the Cominform criticism of Nosaka, the de-Stalinization campaign, and other traumatic events in the Communist world to declare its "independence" of international communism. New student journals of radicalism have made their debut, issuing violent criticism of Khrushchev, and sometimes of Mao Tse-tung as well. Some of these independent elements have been labeled Trotskyites. This Trotskyite faction came to control Zengakuren, and became its Main Current. The Zengakuren anti–Main Current group hewed to the Japanese Communist party line. Throughout the May–June period these two factions were generally in violent opposition.

Because the Communist party maintained that the central foe was American imperialism, it was natural that the students who demonstrated against Eisenhower's press secretary, James Hagerty, were from the anti–Main Current faction of Zengakuren. The Trotskyites, on the other hand, saw the main target as the Kishi government, and consequently kept their atten-

tion focused on the Diet and the anti-Kishi movement. Between
these two elements, bitterness actually increased in the course of
the incidents, and further fragmentation occurred.

Important though the Zengakuren leaders were, there
were other student groups who participated in the post–May 19
demonstrations. Thousands of students from the five Christian
universities in Tokyo paraded, and this was but one example of
nonradical student demonstrators. Subsequent polls revealed that
even a certain number of students favoring the Liberal Democratic
party took part in one or more demonstrations. More impressive,
in some respects, was the response of the mature intellectuals. For
example, some 75 per cent of all faculty members of Tokyo University signed petitions demanding the dissolution of the Diet and
immediate elections. Thousands of intellectuals who had not previously taken an active part in politics suddenly became involved
in protest meetings, petition circulation, and demonstrations before
the Diet and in the Tokyo streets. This, no doubt, acted as an
enormous stimulus to students and to other citizens. Various
occupational groups were organized. Such diverse groups as
housewives, actresses, and Christians were mobilized for protest
purposes.

Organized labor, especially Sōhyō, has represented
another group frequently engaged in political agitation, and, as we
have noted, Sōhyō had been a pioneer in the movement against the
security treaty. But many of the past work stoppages conducted
by Sōhyō had been dreary, ill-supported affairs. In the aftermath
of the May 19 incident, however, on June 4 a stoppage conducted
by the communications workers reportedly involved over five and
one-half million workers, the largest such action in the history of
Japan. Contrary to many earlier occasions, moreover, this work
stoppage seemed to have considerable public sympathy.

Thus Tokyo rocked with demonstrations in the days
that followed May 19. As was noted earlier, this was in many
respects the most impressive mass movement ever witnessed in
modern Japan. Over thirteen million citizens signed petitions urging
Diet dissolution and new elections. Hundreds of thousands of people
marched and demonstrated in Tokyo and other cities. Millions
engaged in work stoppages. Polls indicated that opposition to both

the treaty and the Kishi government was mounting. In July, 1959, for example, a poll indicated that 31 per cent favored a new security treaty with the United States, 28 per cent were opposed, and 41 per cent either did not know or were indifferent. In February, 1960, those who supported ratification of the revised treaty were 25 per cent, those who opposed 36 per cent, and 39 per cent were in the "don't know" or "indifferent" categories. A *Tōkyō Shimbun* poll taken on May 26–27, 1960, indicated that 27 per cent of the people thought the revised treaty necessary, 42 per cent believed it to be unnecessary, 11½ per cent were indifferent, and 17 per cent did not know. In this same poll, 74 per cent of those questioned favored the resignation of the Kishi cabinet, 17 per cent were opposed, and 6½ per cent did not know. Support for the dissolution of the Diet was almost equally heavy. Another poll conducted on June 3 throughout Japan indicated that 58 per cent of the people favored the resignation of the Kishi cabinet, whereas 12 per cent supported its continuance. These polls indicated that, among postwar Japanese cabinets, the Kishi cabinet had reached an all-time low position in terms of public opinion.[6]

The climax to the political unrest was reached between June 10 and 19. The Hagerty incident occurred on June 10, when Press Secretary Hagerty and Ambassador MacArthur were surrounded by Zengakuren (anti–Main Current) demonstrators at the airport, had their car jostled up and down, and finally had to be taken to Tokyo by military helicopter. It is to be noted that no physical violence accompanied this or other incidents up to this

[6] At various times the *Asahi Shimbun* has asked the question, "Do you support the cabinet?" Note the results of a poll taken shortly after the May 19 incident, at the height of unpopularity of the Kishi cabinet, and compare them with the low points of other cabinets:

	YES	No	DON'T KNOW, OR INDIFFERENT
	(Percentage distribution)		
Kishi cabinet (May, 1960)	12	58	30
Hatoyama cabinet (August, 1956)	29	41	30
Yoshida cabinet (May, 1954)	23	48	29
Ashida cabinet (July, 1948)	16	52	32

point. Nor were the majority of demonstrations anti-American; they were anti-Kishi. Americans mingled freely in the crowds, and, often, a holiday mood seemed to prevail. On June 15, however, violence erupted in the vicinity of the Diet. It was initiated by a right-wing extremist group who apparently drove a truck into a line of demonstrators, most of whom were women. Students witnessing the spectacle stormed the Diet gates and clashed with the police. Six hundred students were injured and one woman student was trampled to death in the ensuing struggle. Violence even extended to certain side-line groups. In their excitement, police attacked some university instructors who were seeking to negotiate on behalf of the wounded students, and also attacked some newsmen covering the scene. Once again, as a result of this episode, the Kishi government was bitterly criticized by almost the entire Japanese press. But at the same time the press also began to criticize the anti-government movement for some of the activities taking place.[7]

On June 16, the government was forced to ask for a postponement of President Eisenhower's visit. Opposition to ratification did not cease. On June 19, over three hundred thousand demonstrators surrounded the Diet in a vain effort to demand dissolution, and there were still a hundred thousand standing in front of the building at midnight when the treaty automatically secured Diet approval. Confronted with this *fait accompli*, the demonstrators at last retired; the crisis was over. On June 23, the ratifications were exchanged in Tokyo, and Premier Kishi announced his resignation. The Kishi government stayed in office for another month while maneuvering took place within the Liberal Democratic party to determine the new leadership. Finally, on July 18, Ikeda Hayato was formally elected premier by a special

[7] See Arase Yutaka, "Is Speech Really Free?" *Sekai*, August, 1960, pp. 203–216, and Nakano Yoshio, "Changing Editorial Opinions," *Shisō*, August, 1960, pp. 129–139.

After the June 15 clash between police and students, the press began to voice alarm about violence and unparliamentary activities. On June 17 the seven major newspapers issued a joint statement asserting that, no matter how crucial the causes for which they fought, the socialists should stop denouncing the conservatives and reënter the Diet.

session of the Diet, after having won the presidency of the Liberal Democratic party a few days earlier. A new era had begun.

Let us now return to the questions posed at the beginning of this study. First, why did the Kishi cabinet have to resign when its party, the Liberal Democratic party, commanded an overwhelming majority in the Diet, and why did many of the conservative leaders desert Kishi at this critical period of his career? As we have seen, an answer to this question involves an understanding of the Japanese system of political factions. At no time during the crisis did the majority party act in united fashion. The anti–Main Current factions (Miki-Matsumura, Ishibashi, and Kōno) openly denounced Kishi's tactics, and helped in a variety of ways to strengthen the anti-Kishi front. Even the so-called middle factions (Ikeda, Ōno, and Ishii) although supporting the party and the treaty, directed some criticism against Kishi and Satō for their "highhanded tactics." Thus, within the Liberal Democratic party, the factions of Kishi and his brother, Satō Eisaku, tended to become isolated. This, perhaps more than any other single factor, made Kishi's resignation inevitable.

It might be argued that this situation was produced by the indignation of men who, though they were members of the conservative party, could not approve of the policies being pursued by the current leadership, or, in some cases, were antagonized by the failure of the Kishi-Satō factions to consult them concerning tactics. It might also be argued that many conservatives could not help being impressed and concerned by the trends in the press and in public opinion. There can be no doubt that a certain percentage of demonstrators against Kishi were regular supporters of the Liberal Democratic party. Subsequent polls taken among university and college students in the Tokyo area revealed this fact, and the percentage among other groups was undoubtedly higher in most cases. Despite these factors, however, it remains true that the opposition to Kishi within the Liberal Democratic party ran in accordance with factional lines and general factional positions. The anti-Kishi factions denounced his tactics not so much because they were shocked by government actions as because they wanted to oust Kishi, supplanting him with one of their own leaders.

The Crisis of May-June, 1960

Once again, the supremacy of the faction as the primary unit of political loyalty in Japanese politics was revealed. Thus the loosely knit alliance of conservative factions broke under a political crisis which offered excellent chances of political realignment. Factional divisions, moreover, were equally important in the maneuvering that took place openly after the announcement of Kishi's resignation. The three "middle faction" leaders, Ikeda, Ōno, and Ishii, each began to seek the party presidency and the succession to Kishi as prime minister. Ikeda hoped for the support of the Main Current Kishi-Satō factions, and the possible backing of the Miki-Matsumura faction as well, since in the days prior to the Kishi cabinet reorganization of June, 1959, his faction had been close to this group in an anti-Kishi front.

Ōno also hoped to obtain Kishi-Satō backing, since his faction had given much needed assistance during the controversy over the revised police law in the fall of 1958, as well as in the recent crisis. Ōno, however, also hoped for support from his close friend and fellow "party politician," Kōno, a prominent leader of the anti–Main Current faction. Ishii also hoped to obtain Kishi-Satō support, and emphasized his strong position among conservatives in the House of Councilors.

The position of the Kishi-Satō factions was critical, because despite their recent adversities the two brothers controlled the votes of about one hundred and ten members of the lower house. According to informed political sources, the Kishi-Satō factions wanted the new conservative leader to preside over a five-faction alliance (Kishi, Satō, Ikeda, Ōno, and Ishii), an alliance that would exclude the three anti–Main Current factions (Miki-Matsumura, Kōno, and Ishibashi). They wanted to prevent any Ikeda-Miki or Ōno-Kōno coalition. Reportedly, Kishi spoke to each of the three "middle faction" contenders about the possibility of their becoming prime minister, but he did not initially throw his support to any one man. Kawashima Shōjirō, secretary-general of the party, served as mediator and middleman, in traditional Japanese style.

On June 24 Ikeda received important support from ex-Premier Yoshida. To meet this gain, the Ōno and Ishii forces drew together in a defensive alliance, and the factional struggle was intensified. On July 2 the Liberal Democratic party leadership agreed upon a meeting to decide its next presidency and the prime-ministership on July 13. Negotiations and bargaining were now conducted on a round-the-clock basis. Satō began to visit the three "middle faction" contenders, seeking a compromise solution. On July 6 the three met and decided to leave the decision to a "five-boss conference." But the leaders of the Main Current and middle factions were unable to reach a unanimous decision. Further mediation seemed impossible, and it was decided that the issue should be settled by a party vote. On July 8 and 9, the three contenders announced that they would each stand for the election. In addition, Matsumura (Miki-Matsumura faction) and Foreign Minister Fujiyama (Kishi faction) declared their candidacies.

The contest, however, appeared to be between Ikeda and Ōno. Ōno was now seeking to develop a "party-politician alliance" composed of the Ōno, Ishii, and Kōno factions, while Ikeda, supported by Satō, was seeking to obtain the support of the entire Main Current group and such independent elements as were backing Fujiyama. On July 13 Ōno and Matsumura suddenly withdrew in order to support Ishii as the joint candidate of the "party-politician factions." Kishi now made clear his support of Ikeda. The result of the final ballot was 302 votes for Ikeda to 194 votes for Ishii.[8]

The new Ikeda cabinet represented an alliance of the five factions that the Kishi-Satō groups desired. Four ministers were selected from the Ikeda faction, two from Satō, two from Kishi (with an additional one from the new Fujiyama faction, formerly a branch of the Kishi faction), two from Ōno, and one from Ishii. In addition, two "neutrals" and three House of Councilor independents were selected. With respect to the new party officials, the secretary-general came from the Kishi faction, the

[8] According to Liberal Democratic party rules, the president is elected by a party conference consisting of the party Diet members (at that time 286 representatives and 135 councilors), and prefectural delegates, two from each prefectural federation of party branches (at that time 92).

chairman of the executive board from Satō, the chairman of the policy research committee from Kishi. The anti–Main Current factions were excluded from the cabinet. This was also a signal victory for the ex-official elements; the party-politician factions were given no major posts.[9]

It is because of these facts that the Japanese political factions deserve, in many respects, to be considered as parties in their own right. To be sure, these "parties" are closed, mutual-interest clubs, exclusive in nature. And because the constantly varying combinations of these clubs make up the larger federations which we designate as the Japanese political parties, the latter too partake of the "exclusive club" character.

But, while factional strife played a major role in bringing down the Kishi government, one cannot ignore such other factors as the adamant socialist opposition that helped to produce the May 19 incident and thereby opened the pathway to succeeding events. This again raises the question as to why the Japanese socialists have seemed so ambivalent toward the parliamentary system. Many left-wing socialists of Japan can be called believers in parliamentarism-plus. The "plus" refers to the fact that they are quite willing to go beyond parliamentarism if it does not produce the results they desire. To them, legitimate tactics represent a continuum from the Diet to the streets, from elections to sit-downs, demonstrations, and even violence. Historically, violence and suppression have interacted in Japanese politics, and this may still be a threat. But how is the position of many Japanese socialists to be explained?

The fact that a number of socialists retain a Marxist

[9] *Asahi Shimbun,* July 19, 1960, p. 1. One year earlier, in June, 1959, the Kishi cabinet had consisted of five Kishi faction men, two Satō faction, one Ōno faction, two Kōno faction, two Ikeda faction and three councilors (one Kishi, one Ōno, and one neutral). The secretary-general had been a Kishi faction man, the chairman of the Policy Research Committee an Ōno faction man, and the chairman of the party Executive Committee had been Ishii. Such a cabinet is known in Japanese as *habatsu kinkō naikaku,* "a faction-balanced cabinet." See *Asahi nenkan,* 1960, p. 192.

The Crisis of May-June, 1960

creed is a partial explanation. Marxism legalizes, indeed demands, tactics that go beyond parliamentarism. Especially in its Leninist forms, it is the "science" of the use and abuse of parliamentarism. In addition to this, however, there are other factors, some of them traditionally Japanese. As we noted earlier, majoritarianism is a new theory for Japan, one of dubious validity and ethical worth. Decision making, Japanese style, is based upon consensus. There is still a deep feeling in many quarters that it is immoral and "undemocratic" for a majority to govern, for decisions to be reached without compromise with the minority. Yet, as we have noted, negotiation and compromise in Japanese politics take place almost wholly among factions, not between parties. Between the major parties there is almost no communication. This is partly the result of the wide ideological separation, but it goes beyond this problem. Indeed, the difficulty of intergroup communications is a serious one in all parts of Japanese society. Once again, this seems closely connected with the closed nature of the primary social unit, the leader-follower group. *Japan represents the paradox of an open society made up of closed components.*

Beyond the Marxist and traditional obstacles that cloud socialist acceptance of Western-style parliamentarism and its rules, there also exist certain obstacles mounted by the conservatives. When the political history of modern Japan is viewed in total perspective, are not some doubts about the liberalism of Japanese conservatives in order? Has not their record on behalf of civil liberties and minority rights, thus far, been rather weak? Undoubtedly, most socialists are too quick to see "fascism" and "militarism" under every conservative proposal or action. Perhaps their fears mark them as living in a bygone era, and are partly engendered by the hope of political gain; or perhaps the old refrain is the only one with which they feel comfortable. Yet, whatever the element of change and evolution in postwar Japanese conservatism, many individual Japanese conservatives do remain antiliberal, many abhor the new constitution and regard most, if not all, of the American reforms as ill conceived. They still cherish the hope, quite probably forlorn, of making sweeping changes.

They have had as little experience with genuine debate, and as little trust in Western-style parliamentarism, as their counterparts on the left.

Clearly, there were thousands of articulate non-Marxist Japanese who regarded the tactics of the Kishi government, especially the *fait accompli* of May 19, as a conservative brand of "parliamentarism-plus." This, combined with the deeply rooted intellectual suspicions of Japanese conservatism in general, produced the movement to preserve democracy against the "tyranny of the majority." One of the truly remarkable aspects of the recent crisis was the massive participation of the intellectuals. As has been noted, the journalist world was overwhelmingly anti-Kishi, and the assault of almost all leading newspapers upon the tactics of the Kishi government certainly was important in cultivating mass support for the demonstrations. In addition, hundreds of intellectuals participated in a direct political movement for the first time in their lives.

To abandon the role of scholar encased in the study-cocoon, to *act* instead of merely writing, to translate the role of social critic into that of social actionist—for many intellectuals these were novel and temporarily exhilarating experiences. In the aftermath, some inevitably had doubts, second thoughts, and uncertainties. A note of self-consciousness, even embarrassment, later made its entry into certain intellectual circles. As yet, it is uncertain whether these incidents have marked the beginnings of a deeper commitment on the part of Japanese intellectuals to active political participation. The intellectual cannot be equated with the Socialist party, nor with any organized political group. Yet in some degree, perhaps, he shares the socialist ambivalence concerning Western-style parliamentarism, at least as it operates in Japan. Many of this class feel that the parties and the Diet do not reflect public opinion accurately, that the parties are closed organizations to which the people have no real access, and that elections are won or lost on the basis of funds expended, not on the basis of issues. It is for this reason that some Japanese intellectuals refuse to accept the moral right of the "majority" party. But it is also true that some talk of "qualitative democracy," a term which seeks to differentiate between an articulate elite (naturally, "progressive"), an elite which "knows the political facts of life," and the mass— particularly the rural mass—which is politically ignorant and easily bought or led. In truth, of course, this is an elitist theory or a theory of tutelage, at variance with the concepts of "quantitative" democracy upon which contemporary parliamentary institutions must rest. But it helps to account for such attempts as those by the students to go back to their home districts after the May–June incidents and "educate" the rural voters. It also provides a partial explanation for the feeling of many intellectuals that a great separation exists between the parties and the Diet on the one hand and the real interests of the Japanese people on the other. A very significant number of Japanese intellectuals believed that they were defending democracy in the only manner possible—outside the Diet, and even outside the regular political parties—in a direct appeal to the masses, which was also to serve as a method of education. But it must be recognized that these intellectuals did have as their central demand Diet dissolution and a general election focusing on the treaty revision issue. Thus, whatever their misgivings about the Japanese parliamentary system, the parties, the elections, and the common man, the basic intellectual demand was for a test of public sentiment in conventional fashion—through the ballot.

In the over-all picture of Japanese politics today, however, one fact seems to stand out clearly. Neither major party has any very deep roots among the Japanese people. Even the recent incidents illustrate this point in graphic fashion. Curiously, the Socialist party did not gain popular approval or support in proportion to the loss of strength on the part of the Kishi government. On the whole, the Socialist party displayed itself throughout the crisis as a fundamentally weak party, with shallow mass roots. It did not lead. Nor did the Communist party lead in any real sense. And in the immediate aftermath of the crisis, one poll indicated that both major parties, *including the Socialists*, had declined somewhat in popular support.[10] In short, whatever else may be

[10] Note the following very interesting polls conducted by the *Asahi Shimbun:*
On May 25 and 26 the question was asked: "What do you think

faulty in the Japanese intellectuals' current analysis of democratic weaknesses in their society, their thesis of a substantial separation between the parties and Diet on the one hand and the broad public on the other has some validity. And this is why no immediate or startling changes are likely to take place in the relative standing of the parties. But this is also why political stability in contemporary Japan is a somewhat deceptive phenomenon.

---

about the activities of the conservatives (the government), the socialists, and the democratic socialists?" The results were as follows, in percentages:

	"Good"	"Bad"	"Neither good nor bad"
Conservatives (government)	6	50	18
Socialists	11	32	31
Democratic Socialists	8	13	43

When asked which party the interviewee supported, another *Asahi Shimbun* poll gave the following percentage results in May, 1960, which can be compared with results in January, 1960, and earlier:

	May, 1960	Jan., 1960	Feb., 1959	Sept., 1958	Nov., 1957	July, 1957	Mar., 1956	Dec., 1956	Aug., 1956
Liberal Democratic	40	48	48	46	45	47	46	48	45
Socialist	30	31	36	33	33	32	33	34	39
Democratic Socialist	9	4	...	...	...	...	...	...	...
Communist	1	0	0	0	0	1	1	0	0
No party	7	5	4	4	5	5	6	4	4
No answer	13	12	12	12	16	15	14	14	12

And in August, two months after the incident, in an *Asahi* poll asking the same question the percentages showed the Socialists at a new low, with the Democratic Liberals having gained, possibly as a result of the conciliatory statements and gestures of the new prime minister, Ikeda:

Liberal Democratic	49
Socialist	25
Democratic Socialist	6
Communist	...
No party	8
No answer	12

This poll was reasonably close to the November, 1960, election results, when the "undecided–don't know" vote is prorated. *Asahi Shimbun,* August 8, 1960, p. 1.

The Crisis of May-June, 1960

In summation, there is considerable truth in the thesis that Japanese democratic institutions—the complex of parties, and parliament—have not yet been meshed very effectively with the broader patterns of rapid socioeconomic change that characterize this society. Indeed, the persistence of old political behavior and old organizational molds seems to belie the new institutions that were bequeathed Japan by American innovators. In these senses, socioeconomic changes have been moving much more rapidly than political ones. One must presume that there will be a day of reckoning. Perhaps in some measure the May–June incidents were the beginning of that day. As we suggested earlier, they represented a degree of mass participation (and one might say even more accurately, a degree of elitist participation) in some respects unparalleled in Japanese domestic politics. It is unclear, of course, whether that participation will be sustained in some fashion. Will it be nourished, and will it grow? One is aware that the "mass" element was largely confined to Tokyo and a few other large cities, and that the rural areas took relatively little part.[11] Once again, the striking political differences between metropolitan and rural areas were clearly revealed.

The basic issue, however, revolves around the question of how Japanese political processes and institutions will adjust to the new era of the mass society. The future is not easy to predict. The path ahead is strewn with boulders. As they have been structured in the past, the Japanese parties have not been suitable mass instruments. Essentially, they have been "cadre" or "Diet" parties, with very shallow grass roots. In many respects, the basic political organization has been the faction, not the party. The faction, reflective of the cultural roots of Japanese society and the nature of all Japanese organization, has occupied the vital center of the political process. For this reason, we have suggested that perhaps

[11] For two articles on the relation between the rural areas and the incident, and also the later attempt of the students to "educate" the farmers, see Fukutake Naoshi, "The Village and Democracy," *Sekai,* September, 1960, pp. 38–45 and Fukutake Naoshi *et al.,* "The Actual Condition of the 'Voiceless Voice' in the Village," *Shisō,* October, 1960, pp. 66–78.

the most accurate description of the Japanese party system is that of two relatively stable (and unequal) federations, with each having an internal fluidity as a result of constantly shifting factional coalitions that give Japanese politics its element of suspense and change. In a broader functional sense, of course, this is a one-and-one-half-party system, with a permanent conservative majority.

The danger, however, lies in the fact that no matter how one defines the Japanese party system, up to date it has been essentially a closed system. The parliamentary process in Japan has not sufficiently encompassed the people. The parties continue in large measure to be "they" as opposed to "we" in the popular mind. Under such circumstances, mass participation is likely to operate outside party-Diet channels, as it did recently. This is conducive to variant (and, from a Western perspective, one would say questionable) theories of democracy. The left socialists are encouraged to go on holding their theory of "parliamentarism-plus"; a number of intellectuals believe in "qualitative democracy" (as do others on the right, from a different perspective); and it becomes easier to challenge majoritarianism if, in addition to a traditional practice of consensus that still commands great respect, one has reason to question the bases upon which a majority was obtained.

Yet, viewed from the democratic standpoint, there is some light on the Japanese political horizon. The emergence of multiple-interest groups, mass based and operating on behalf of self-interests, has been one of the truly important developments of postwar Japanese politics. Through these interest groups, many of them new, an ever growing number of Japanese citizens are participating in politics, and affiliating—at least, indirectly—with parties. In spite of the fact that such representation is still woefully unequal and insufficient, and in spite of the fact also that Japanese interest groups have structural and other problems derivative from their culture, the growth of interest group politics may represent the most suitable route to Japanese democracy.

The major parties, moreover, have taken increasing cognizance of the individual voter. They have shown some serious interest in having him join party ranks. They have campaigned with increasing vigor for his vote, and used more direct means, relying less upon intermediaries. The mass media have been utilized to educate the voter, and party leaders have stumped the nation in a fashion that would have astounded most politicians of the prewar era. And when the voters' position on an issue is made clear by means of accepted polls, the politicians generally pay some heed—at least, to the extent of changing the pace or modifying the stance. Polling has become a supplement to elections in the cause of Japanese democracy, the more important perhaps because elections are not necessarily an accurate gauge of public opinion.

Even with respect to voting behavior, however, a significant transition seems to be under way. The shift is from the "traditional" to the "modern" behavior: from voting as a method of ratifying authority to voting as a means of expressing one's needs and values. This transition is by no means complete. Traditional patterns are still very strong, especially in the rural areas, but all political elements in Japan are conscious of the change that is taking place.

In some respects, curiously enough, it is the conservatives rather than the "progressives" who have thus far shown the greater flexibility in connection with the new age.[12] The Japanese socialists run some risk of being considered by history the real conservatives of this era, unable to evolve and frozen in impotence. Continuity in power has given the conservatives an important advantage in adjusting to the changing requirements of power, and continuity out of power has heightened the socialist problem of moving from the world of the past into that of the present and future. It is easy to say that the Japanese socialists should become "more responsible." But how? How does a party become responsible without power and, indeed, when it is almost without hope of

[12] This theme was developed in Robert A. Scalapino, "Japanese Socialism in Crisis," *Foreign Affairs,* January, 1960, pp. 318–328. We have borrowed extensively from the language used there in setting forth the concept.

power? If there is no legacy of policy to defend, irresponsibility is an omnipresent danger; the longer a party is separated from power, the greater the temptations are likely to become.

Will the Japanese conservatives, in the pattern of the conservative parties of western Europe and the United States, become truly progressive conservatives? And if so, will they retain power indefinitely? These questions raise some interesting thoughts that go far beyond Japan in their possible application. We are at a juncture in history when the "advanced" societies have accomplished, or are en route to accomplishing, many of the basic goals of democratic socialism, albeit often under different designations. Is it possible that progressive conservatives can conduct a "permanent revolution" with sufficient skill to keep the opposition out of power indefinitely? Needless to say, this would not be Trotsky's permanent revolution, but rather one in which the conservatives adjusted to the importance of the mass man, acknowledged and anticipated his most basic needs, and attuned organizational attention upon him with sufficient skill to put the opposition (however "mass oriented" in an ideological sense) indefinitely on the defensive.

Perhaps such a "permanent revolution" is not entirely possible, either in Japan or elsewhere. A depression might suddenly alter the picture—if it could not be modified by the government in power. Long continuity in power can lead to complacency, corruption, or grievous errors and thereby produce a mood for change. But there have been enough advances in the science of power and in socioeconomic trends in the "advanced" world, of which Japan is now a part, to suggest a new problem for democracy: the problem of the perennial minority. Democracy is in peril if one party knows only how to govern and the others only how to oppose.

In political terms, however, Japan does not yet belong wholly to the "advanced" world, and the above concern is in certain respects premature. Mass participation in Japanese politics is on the rise. Party policies and organization are increasingly attuned to the fact. Political behavior shows various signs of moving away from traditionalism and toward modernity. However, in

The Crisis of May-June, 1960

comparison with the startling rapidity that has characterized socio-economic change in postwar Japan, political change has been extremely slow and uneven. Traditional patterns of organization and process are omnipresent. Any society undergoing a very rapid transformation faces serious problems in keeping its various elements in balance. Socioeconomic change may take place at a pace much accelerated over that of political change. As the imbalance between *politics* and *society* mounts, the situation becomes increasingly explosive.

There is no question that Japan is proceeding to the status of a mass society. Mass participation in politics will steadily increase. In this sense, the May–June incidents are symptomatic of a new era. But, will this participation find channels of expression within the parliamentary process? Will the Japanese people, maturing as a result of educational expansion and economic growth, develop the type of complex, mass-based interest group structure that can reflect more fully the desires and needs of the total population and be used to pry open the exclusive nature of Japanese political organization? Will political leadership in Japan anticipate more adequately the requirements of a democratic mass society? Can the tempo of political change in modern Japan be advanced? If not, many dangers lie ahead. Mass participation, as in the case of the May–June incidents, can circumvent parties and parliament, causing them to stand impotent and alone. Such participation can take the form of "to the streets" on the left and "via the knife" on the right. The paradox of Japan's being an open society made up of closed components must be ended. Otherwise, many perils lie ahead. And it is for these reasons that Japanese politics is both stable and unstable, depending upon how deeply one wishes to probe.

APPENDIX

Appendix

Chart 1.   THE JAPANESE ELECTORATE

Date	Total Electors	Index of Increase	Total Voters	Voting Percentages	Invalid Votes	Percentage of Invalid
Apr. 10, 1946	36,878,420	100.0	26,582,175	72.08	482,000	1.81
Apr. 25, 1947	40,907,493	110.9	27,797,748	67.95	435,180	1.57
Jan. 23, 1949	42,105,300	114.2	31,175,895	74.04	582,438	1.87
Oct. 1, 1952	46,772,584	126.8	35,749,723	76.43	412,349	1.15
Apr. 9, 1953	47,090,167	127.7	34,948,008	74.22	342,675	0.98
Feb. 27, 1955	49,235,375	133.5	37,338,021	75.84	319,499	0.86
May 22, 1958	52,013,529	141.0	40,045,111	76.99	290,824	0.73
Nov. 20, 1960	56,554,475	153.4	39,923,232	70.59	410,997	1.03

Source: Compiled from statistics obtained from Election Bureau, Local Autonomy Agency, Office of the Prime Minister.

Chart 2. HOUSE OF REPRESENTATIVES ELECTIONS, 1946–1958 (Figures in parentheses indicate per cent)

Date	Progressive	Liberal	Socialist	Labor-Farmer	Communist	Coöperative	Misc.	Independent	Total
Apr. 10, 1946	10,350,530 (18.7)	13,505,746 (24.4)	9,858,408 (17.8)	...	2,135,757 (3.8)	1,799,764 (3.2)	6,473,272 (11.7)	11,325,402 (20.4)	55,448,879 (100.0)
Apr. 25, 1947	Democratic 6,839,646 (25.0)	7,356,321 (26.9)	7,175,939 (26.2)	...	1,002,903 (3.7)	Natl. Coöp. 1,915,947 (7.0)	1,490,057 (5.4)	1,580,844 (5.8)	27,361,657 (100.0)
Jan. 23, 1949	Democratic 4,798,352 (15.7)	Democratic Liberal 13,420,209 (43.9)	4,129,794 (13.5)	606,840 (2.0)	2,984,780 (9.7)	1,041,879 (3.4)	1,602,496 (5.2)	2,008,109 (6.6)	30,592,519 (100.0)
Oct. 1, 1952	Reform 6,429,450 (18.2)	Liberal 16,938,221 (47.9)	Left 3,398,597 (9.6) Right 4,108,274 (11.6)	261,190 (0.7)	896,765 (2.6)	...	949,036 (2.7)	2,355,172 (6.7)	35,336,705 (100.0)
Apr. 19, 1953	Reform 6,186,232 (17.9)	Hatoyama 3,054,688 (8.8) Yoshida 13,476,428 (39.0)	Left 4,516,715 (13.1) Right 4,677,833 (13.5)	358,773 (1.0)	655,990 (1.9)	...	152,050 (0.4)	1,523,736 (4.4)	34,602,445 (100.0)
Feb. 27, 1955	Democratic 13,536,044.4 (36.6)	Liberal 9,849,457.6 (26.6)	Left 5,683,312 (15.3) Right 5,129,594.3 (13.9)	357,611 (1.0)	733,121.9 (2.0)	...	496,614.4 (1.3)	1,229,081.7 (3.3)	37,014,837.3 (100.0)
May 22, 1958	Liberal Democratic 22,976,846.28 (57.8)		Socialist 13,093,993.10 (32.9)		1,012,035.52 (2.6)	...	278,991.08 (0.7)	2,380,795.21 (6.0)	39,751,661.19 (100.0)
Nov. 20, 1960	Liberal Democratic 22,740,265 (57.6)		Socialists 10,887,137 (27.6)	Democratic Socialist 3,464,147 (8.8)	1,156,723 (2.9)	...	141,941 (0.4)	1,118,908 (2.8)	39,509,121 (100.0)

Source: Compiled from statistics obtained from Election Bureau, Local Autonomy Agency.

Chart 3. ELECTED PERSONS, BY PARTIES (Figures in parentheses indicate per cent)

Date	Progressive	Liberal	Socialist	Labor-Farmer	Communist	Coöperative	Misc.	Independent	Total
Apr. 10, 1946	94 (20.3)	140 (30.2)	92 (19.8)	...	5 (1.1)	14 (3.0)	38 (8.2)	81 (17.4)	464* (100.0)
Apr. 25, 1947	Democratic 121 (26.0)	131 (28.1)	143 (30.7)	...	4 (0.8)	Natl. Coöp. 29 (6.2)	25 (5.4)	13 (2.8)	466 (100.0)
Jan. 23, 1949	69 (14.8)	Democratic Liberal 264 (56.7)	48 (10.3)	7 (1.5)	35 (7.5)	14 (3.0)	17 (3.6)	12 (2.6)	466 (100.0)
Oct. 1, 1952	Reform 85 (18.2)	240 (51.4)	Left 54 (11.6) — Right 57 (12.2)	4 (0.9)	...	...	7 (1.5)	19 (4.1)	466 (100.0)
Apr. 19, 1953	76 (16.3)	Hatoyama 35 (7.5) — Yoshida 199 (42.7)	Left 72 (15.4) — Right 66 (14.2)	5 (1.1)	1 (0.2)	...	1 (0.2)	11 (2.4)	466 (100.0)
Feb. 27, 1955	Democratic 185 (39.6)	Liberal 112 (24.0)	Left 89 (19.1) — Right 67 (14.3)	4 (0.9)	2 (0.4)	...	2 (0.4)	6 (1.3)	467 (100.0)
May 22, 1958	Liberal Democratic 287 (61.5)		Socialist 166 (35.5)		1 (0.2)	...	1 (0.2)	12 (2.6)	467 (100.0)
Nov. 20, 1960	Liberal Democratic 296 (63.4)		Socialist 145 (31)	Democratic Socialist 17 (3.7)	3 (0.6)	...	1 (0.2)	5 (1.1)	467 (100.0)

* In 1946, 464 persons were elected because in the Second District of Tokyo and Fukui the number elected did not reach that fixed by law.
Source: Compiled from statistics obtained from Election Bureau, Local Autonomy Agency.

Chart 4.   NUMBER OF CANDIDATES, BY PARTIES (Figures in parentheses indicate per cent)

Date	Progressive	Liberal	Socialist	Labor-Farmer	Communist	Coöperative	Misc.	Independent	Total	Competitive Rate
Apr., 1946	376 (13.6)	485 (17.5)	331 (11.9)	...	143 (5.2)	92 (3.3)	570 (20.6)	773 (27.9)	2,770 (100.0)	5.9
Apr., 1947	Democratic 350 (22.0)	326 (20.5)	289 (18.2)	...	120 (7.5)	Natl. Coöp. 108 (6.8)	155 (9.8)	242 (15.2)	1,590 (100.0)	3.4
Jan., 1949	208 (15.3)	Democratic Liberal 420 (30.8)	187 (13.7)	45 (3.3)	115 (8.4)	63 (4.6)	115 (8.4)	211 (15.5)	1,364 (100.0)	2.9
Oct., 1952	Reform 209 (16.8)	Liberal 475 (38.2)	Left 96 (7.7) | Right 109 (8.8)	11 (0.9)	107 (8.6)	...	69 (5.6)	166 (13.4)	1,242 (100.0)	2.7
Apr., 1953	169 (16.4)	Hatoyama 102 (9.9) | Yoshida 316 (30.8)	Left 108 (10.5) | Right 117 (11.4)	12 (1.2)	85 (8.3)	...	13 (1.3)	105 (10.2)	1,027 (100.0)	2.2
Feb., 1955	Democratic 286 (28.1)	Liberal 248 (24.4)	Left 121 (11.9) | Right 122 (12.0)	16 (1.6)	60 (5.9)	...	37 (3.6)	127 (12.5)	1,017 (100.0)	2.2
May, 1958	Liberal Democratic 413 (43.4)		Socialist 246 (25.9)		114 (12.0)	...	33 (3.5)	145 (15.2)	951 (100.0)	2.0
Nov., 1960	399 (42.4)		Socialist 186 (19.8)	Social Democratic 105 (11.2)	118 (12.6)	...	34 (3.6)	98 (10.4)	940 (100.0)	2.0

Source: Compiled from statistics obtained from Election Bureau, Local Autonomy Agency.

Chart 5. CANDIDATES NOT PREVIOUSLY IN THE DIET, CANDIDATES CURRENTLY IN THE DIET, AND CANDIDATES PREVIOUSLY IN THE DIET (Figures in parentheses indicate per cent)

Previous Experience	April, 1946		April, 1947		January, 1949		October, 1952		April, 1953		February, 1955		May, 1958		November, 1960	
	C	E	C	E	C	E	C	E	C	E	C	E	C	E	C	E
Not previously in Diet	...	377 (81.3)	...	222 (47.6)	865 (63.4)	192 (41.2)	539 (43.4)	116 (24.9)	332 (32.3)	47 (10.1)	360 (35.4)	55 (11.8)	353 (37.1)	66 (14.1)	376 (40.0)	60 (12.8)
Currently in Diet	...	39 (8.4)	...	237 (50.9)	424 (31.1)	240 (51.5)	400 (32.2)	212 (45.5)	450 (43.8)	329 (70.6)	446 (43.9)	309 (66.2)	449 (47.2)	337 (72.2)	439 (46.7)	344 (73.7)
Previously in Diet	...	48 (10.3)	...	7 (1.5)	75 (5.5)	34 (7.3)	303 (24.4)	138 (29.6)	245 (23.9)	90 (19.3)	211 (20.7)	103 (22.0)	149 (15.7)	64 (13.7)	125 (13.3)	63 (13.5)
Total	2,770	464	1,590	466	1,364	466	1,242	466	1,027	466	1,017	467	951	467	940	467
	(100.0)	(100.0)	(130.0)	(100.0)	(100.0)	(100.0)	(100.0)	(100.0)	(100.0)	(100.0)	(100.0)	(100.0)	(100.0)	(100.0)	(100.0)	(100.0)

Source: Compiled from statistics obtained from Election Bureau, Local Autonomy Agency.
Note: C = Candidates; E = Elected.

Appendix

Chart 6.   TYPES OF CANDIDATES IN JAPANESE ELECTIONS,
1946–1960

Elections	Candidates		Elected Representatives	
April, 1946	A	2,770 (5.9 times)	D	377 (81%)
	B	2,624 (95%)	E	133 (29%)
	C	1,435 (52%)		
April, 1947	A	1,590 (3.4 times)	D	222 (48%)
	B	... (80%)	E	67 (14%)
	C	505 (32%)		
January, 1949	A	1,364 (2.9 times)	D	192 (41%)
	B	865 (63%)	E	50 (11%)
	C	269 (19%)		
October, 1952	A	1,242 (2.7 times)	D	116 (25%)
	B	539 (43%)	E	30 (7%)
	C	182 (11%)		
April, 1953	A	1,027 (2.2 times)	D	47 (10%)
	B	332 (32%)	E	17 (4%)
	C	130 (12%)		
February, 1955	A	1,017 (2.2 times)	D	55 (12%)
	B	360 (35%)	E	12 (3%)
	C	164 (16%)		
May, 1958	A	951 (2.0 times)	D	66 (14%)
	B	353 (37%)	E	13 (3%)
	C	178 (19%)		
November, 1960	A	940 (2.0 times)	D	60 (13%)
	B	376 (40%)	E	6 (1%)
	C	132 (14%)		

Source: H. Fujiwara, *General Elections Handbook*, Tokyo, 1959, and statistics obtained from Election Bureau, Local Autonomy Agency.

A: Total number of candidates.
B: Candidates not previously in the Diet.
C: Independent or minor party candidates.
D: Representatives elected for the first time.
E: Independent or minor party representatives.

Appendix

Chart 7.   GENERAL POLITICAL DISTRIBUTION
OF THE JAPANESE VOTE

Year of Election	"Conservatives"		"Progressives" *	Others
1946	A	53.4%	20.9%	25.6%
	B	46.3%	21.7%	32.1%
1947	A	60.3%	31.5%	8.2%
	B	58.9%	29.9%	11.2%
1949	A	74.5%	20.4%	5.1%
	B	63.0%	26.6%	10.5%
1952	A	69.7%	24.7%	5.6%
	B	66.1%	24.4%	9.4%
1953	A	66.5%	30.9%	2.6%
	B	65.7%	29.5%	4.8%
1955	A	63.6%	34.7%	1.7%
	B	63.2%	32.2%	4.6%
1958	A	61.5%	35.8%	2.8%
	B	57.8%	35.5%	6.7%
1960	A	63.4%	35.4%	1.2%
	B	57.6%	39.2%	3.2%

Source: Fujiwara, *op. cit.*, pp. 383, 385, and Election Bureau, Local Autonomy
Agency.

A: seats; *B*: votes.
* "Progressive" refers to the Socialist party and other "left" parties.

Appendix

Chart 8.   SOCIOECONOMIC COMPOSITION OF HOUSE

OF REPRESENTATIVES (In number of members and

per cent of membership)

1947	Liberal Party		Democratic Party (Progressive Party)		Socialist Party	
Total	120	100%	106	100%	139	100%
Ex-officials	17	14%	8	8%	3	2%
Ex-prefectural assemblymen	35	29%	23	22%	34	24%
Ex-elected local officials	22	18%	33	31%	43	31%
Total[a]	48	40%	42	40%	53	38%
Graduates of national or public universities or colleges	34	28%	22	21%	43	31%
Graduates of private universities or colleges	55	46%	41	39%	37	27%
Business presidents, auditors, or members of boards of directors	66	55%	61	58%	37	27%
General business affiliations	12	10%	25	24%	10	7%
Total[a]	68	57%	68	64%	43	31%
Agricultural Coöperative Association leaders	0	...	2	2%	0	...
General agricultural affiliations	23	19%	16	15%	13	9%
Total[a]	23	19%	17	16%	13	9%
Labor union leaders and affiliated members	0	...	1	1%	42	30%
Farm union leaders and affiliated members	0	...	2	2%	44	32%
Total[a]	0	...	3	3%	72	52%
Times elected (average)	2.1		2.2		1.7	

Appendix

Chart 8.   (*Continued*)

1949	Liberal Democratic Party		Democratic Party		Socialist Party	
Total	261	100%	75	100%	46	100%
Ex-officials	44	17%	13	17%	0	...
Ex-prefectural assemblymen	55	21%	19	25%	11	24%
Ex-elected local officials	67	26%	23	31%	17	37%
Total*	91	35%	29	39%	20	43%
Graduates of national or public universities or colleges	86	33%	27	36%	12	26%
Graduates of private universities or colleges	100	38%	27	36%	16	35%
Business presidents, auditors, or members of boards of directors	158	61%	50	67%	10	22%
General business affiliations	61	23%	22	29%	5	11%
Total*	166	64%	53	70%	13	28%
Agricultural Coöperative Association leaders	16	6%	5	7%	1	2%
General agricultural affiliations	32	12%	7	9%	1	2%
Total*	44	17%	10	13%	2	4%
Labor union leaders and affiliated members	1		1	...	16	35%
Farm union leaders and affiliated members	0	...	1	...	10	22%
Total*	1	...	2	...	21	46%
Times elected (average)	2.1		2.2		2.6	

Appendix

Chart 8.   (*Continued*)

1953	Liberal Party		Reform Party		Socialist Party (Right)		Socialist Party (Left)	
Total	237	100%	76	100%	66	100%	71	100%
Ex-officials	58	25%	14	18%	2	3%	1	...
Ex-prefectural assemblymen	56	24%	14	18%	20	30%	3	4%
Ex-elected officials	63	27%	17	22%	25	38%	19	27%
Total[a]	83	35%	24	32%	32	49%	23	31%
Graduates of national or public universities or colleges	107	45%	33	44%	18	27%	18	25%
Graduates of private universities or colleges	88	37%	30	40%	29	44%	20	28%
Business presidents, auditors, or members of boards of directors	152	64%	46	61%	20	30%	13	18%
General business affiliations	39	16%	13	17%	8	12%	5	7%
Total[a]	159	67%	46	61%	23	35%	17	24%
Agricultural Coöperative Association leaders	21	9%	7	9%	2	3%	4	6%
General agricultural affiliations	19	8%	4	5%	1	...	1	...
Total[a]	38	16%	11	14%	3	5%	5	7%
Labor union leaders and affiliated members	0	...	0	...	21	32%	19	27%
Farm union leaders and affiliated members	0	...	1	...	19	29%	12	17%
Total[a]	0	...	1	...	33	50%	30	42%
Times elected (average)	3.8		3.5		3.8		2.5	

Appendix

Chart 8.   (*Continued*)

1958	Liberal Democratic Party		Socialist Party	
Total	298	100%	168	100%
Ex-officials	79	26%	7	4%
Ex-prefectural assemblymen	55	18%	45	27%
Ex-elected local officials	78	26%	49	29%
Total[a]	100	34%	70	41%
Graduates of national or public universities or colleges	143	48%	49	30%
Graduates of private universities or colleges	97	33%	54	32%
Business presidents, auditors, or members of boards of directors	144	48%	26	14%
General business affiliations	35	12%	10	6%
Total[a]	156	52%	31	18%
Agricultural Coöperative Association leaders	17	6%	14	8%
General agricultural affiliations	48	16%	4	2%
Total[a]	58	19%	17	10%
Labor union leaders and affiliated members	0	. . .	55	33%
Farm union leaders and affiliated members	1	. . .	33	20%
Total[a]	1	. . .	84	50%
Times elected (average)	4.6		3.8	

Source: *Shugiin Yōran* ("House of Representatives Survey") 1947, 1949, 1953, 1958.

[a] The totals in these columns are adjusted to account for members with dual affiliations.

Appendix

Chart 9.   CABINET COMPOSITION, 1948–1960

Cabinet	Number of Cabinet Members	Members of the House of Councilors	Members of the House of Representatives	Exofficials	Exprefectural Assemblymen
2d Yoshida Oct. 15, 1948	15	1	11	5	5
3d Yoshida Feb. 16, 1949	17	2	14	6	6
5th Yoshida May 21, 1953	18	4	14	6	2
1st Hatoyama Dec. 10, 1954	18	3	13	5	4
2d Hatoyama Mar. 19, 1955	18	2	16	5	3
3d Hatoyama Nov. 22, 1955	19	2	16	7	3
Ishibashi Dec. 23, 1956	15	0	15	4	2
Reformed Kishi July 10, 1957	18	1	15	9	2
2d Kishi June 13, 1958	18	2	15	8	2
Reformed 2d Kishi June 18, 1959	18	2	15	9	1
2d Ikeda Dec. 8, 1960	17	3	14	9	. . .

Source: Compiled on the basis of data given in *Asahi nenkan* ("*Asahi* Yearbook"), 1959, pp. 219-221; 1960, pp. 229-231; 1961, pp. 225-226.

Chart 10. FACTIONAL COMPOSITION OF THE LIBERAL DEMOCRATIC PARTY AS COMPILED BY VARIOUS SOURCES

Source	Date	Kishi	Satō	Ikeda	Ishii	Ōno	Kōno	Miki-Matsumura	Ishi-bashi	Others	Fuji-yama[h]
Kanchō monogatari[a]	Mar., 1958	50	24	25	34	28	35	40	17	...	
Shūkan Asahi[b]	Feb., 1958	...	...	51	26	...	...	37	10	...	
Yomiuri[c]	May, 1958	70	28	28	22	28	40	40	17	...	
Sankei[d]	May-June, 1958	70	30	28	...	30	...	...	...	...	
	May, 1958, Election										
Yomiuri[c]	May, 1958	54	36	40	22	35	33	34	14	24	
Tōkyō[e]	May, 1958	65	33	48	25	37	34	33	16	...	
Nihon Keizai[f]	May, 1958	63	34	47	20	34	37	31	16	...	
Sankei[d]	May-June, 1958	60	40	50	24	40	30	32	20	...	
Habatsu[g]	Sept., 1958	56	41	38	22	44	36	35	15	28	
Shūkan Asahi[b]	Jan., 1960	60	40	40	20	30	40	30	...	...	
Anonymous	Jan., 1960	60	38	48	18	32	32	29	29	24	
	November, 1960, Election										
Mainichi[i]	Nov., 1960	50	49	52	17	28	32	31	...	9	28
Asahi[j]	Nov., 1960	45	46	54	16	26	35	27	...	17	34

Note: Most of these sources, it will be noted, are newspapers which maintain a staff of political writers constantly checking political trends. This chart gives an idea of the range of estimates made by relatively reliable sources.

a Kanchō monogatari ("Stories of Government Office") (Tokyo: Tōkyō Shimbun, 1958).
b Shūkan Asahi ("Asahi Weekly").
c Yomiuri Shimbun.
d Sankei Shimbun.
e Tōkyō Shimbun.
f Nihon Keizai ("Japan Economist")
g Watanabe Tsuneo, Habatsu ("The Cliques") (Tokyo, 1958).
h The Fujiyama faction was previously a part of the Kishi faction, but since the fall of the Kishi government it has acquired an independent status.
i Mainichi Shimbun.
j Asahi Shimbun.

Chart 11.   Factional Composition of the Socialist Party as Compiled by Various Sources

Source	Date	Nishio	Kawakami	Suzuki	Wada	Nomizo	Matsumoto*	Kuroda*	Others
Kanchō monogatari[a]	Mar., 1958	15	43	32	20	4	12	...	20
Sankei[b]	May-June, 1958	...	44	41	...	...	...	...	...
				May, 1958, Election					
Yomiuri[c]	May, 1958	12	51	51	17	6	13	6	11
Tōkyō[d]	May, 1958	27	29	40	29	5	12	5	...
Nihon Keizai[e]	May, 1958	22	42	39	33	5	9	5	...
Sankei[b]	May-June, 1958	16	48	45	24	7	15	6	4
				October, 1958, Split					
		Democratic Socialist Party							
Anonymous	Oct., 1958	21	...	...	...	...	...	...	...
	Jan., 1960	35	32	39	30	4	14	6	5
Private source	May, 1960	40	27	39	32	...	14	6	7
				November, 1960, Election					
Mainichi[f]	1960	17	28	56	28	7	13	...	10

* Matsumoto and Kuroda factions are also called "Heiwa-dōshi-kai" ("Peace Comrades' Association") and "Rōnō-ha" ("Workers' and Farmers' Faction"), respectively.
a Kanchō monogatari ("Stories of Government Office") (Tokyo: Tōkyō Shimbun, 1958).
b Sankei Shimbun.
c Yomiuri Shimbun.
d Tōkyō Shimbun.
e Nihon Keizai ("Japan Economist").
f Mainichi Shimbun.

Chart 12. Liberal Democratic Party Factions and Their Socioeconomic Composition

(In number of members and percentage distribution)

Composition		Kishi		Satō		Ikeda		Ishii		Miki-Matsumura		Ōno		Kōno		Ishibashi		Total	
Number of members	A	54	100%	36	100%	33	100%	22	100%	34	100%	37	100%	33	100%	14	100%	298	100%
	B	65	100%	33	100%	48	100%	25	100%	33	100%	37	100%	33	100%	16	100%		
	C	56	100%	41	100%	37	100%	22	100%	35	100%	44	100%	36	100%	15	100%		
Ex-officials	A	19	35%	13	36%	14	43%	8	36%	6	18%	5	14%	5	15%	1	7%	79	26%
	B	23	35%	11	33%	17	35%	9	36%	6	16%	4	11%	6	18%	2	13%		
	C	18	32%	13	32%	15	41%	7	32%	6	17%	6	(14%)	5	14%	2	13%		
Ex-prefectural assemblymen	A	11	9%	5	14%	4	12%	4	18%	4	12%	5	14%	9	27%	2	14%	55	18%
	B	13	20%	5	15%	8	17%	3	12%	4	12%	6	16%	9	27%	3	19%		
	C	11	20%	6	15%	5	14%	5	23%	4	11%	7	16%	11	31%	3	20%		
Ex-elected local officials	A	14	26%	7	20%	7	21%	6	27%	9	26%	12	32%	9	27%	4	29%	78	26%
	B	14	22%	8	24%	13	27%	4	16%	9	27%	12	32%	8	24%	4	25%		
	C	14	25%	7	17%	10	27%	6	27%	10	29%	11	25%	11	31%	4	27%		
Total[a] ex-prefectural assemblymen and ex-elected local officials	A	16	30%	10	28%	10	30%	6	27%	10	29%	14	38%	14	40%	5	36%	100	34%
	B	17	26%	11	33%	17	35%	5	20%	10	30%	15	41%	14	40%	5	31%		
	C	16	29%	10	24%	13	35%	7	32%	11	31%	16	36%	16	45%	5	33%		
Graduates of national or public universities or colleges	A	31	57%	18	50%	21	64%	11	50%	15	44%	16	43%	10	30%	4	29%	143	48%
	B	36	55%	17	51%	29	61%	11	44%	14	43%	16	43%	10	30%	5	31%		
	C	31	55%	21	51%	21	57%	11	50%	13	37%	19	43%	11	31%	5	33%		
Graduates of private universities or colleges[b]	A	14	26%	11	31%	6	18%	9	41%	12	35%	16	43%	13	40%	7	50%	97	33%
	B	20	31%	7	21%	12	25%	11	44%	11	33%	16	43%	12	36%	6	38%		
	C	16	29%	12	29%	9	24%	9	36%	14	40%	19	43%	15	42%	7	47%		
Business presidents, auditors, or members of boards of directors	A	31	57%	15	42%	21	64%	13	69%	11	32%	21	57%	14	43%	7	50%	144	43%
	B	37	57%	14	43%	32	67%	14	56%	10	30%	20	54%	13	40%	9	56%		
	C	31	55%	19	46%	22	60%	13	69%	11	31%	25	57%	15	42%	8	53%		

Chart 12.   (Continued)

Composition		Kishi	Satō	Ikeda	Ishii	Miki-Matsumura	Ōno	Kōno	Ishibashi	Total
General business affiliations	A	13 24%	2 6%	3 9%	1 5%	3 9%	5 14%	3 9%	2 14%	35 12%
	B	10 15%	2 6%	7 15%	2 8%	4 12%	4 11%	3 9%	2 13%	
	C	13 23%	3 7%	4 11%	1 5%	3 ...	5 11%	4 11%	2 13%	
Total	A	35 65%	17 47%	22 67%	14 64%	12 35%	22 60%	15 46%	8 52%	156 52%
	B	39 60%	16 49%	34 71%	15 60%	12 36%	21 57%	14 43%	10 63%	
	C	35 63%	21 51%	23 62%	14 64%	12 34%	26 59%	16 45%	9 60%	
Agricultural Coöperative Association leaders	A	5 9%	2 6%	0 ...	0 ...	4 12%	1 3%	1 3%	0 ...	17 6%
	B	4 6%	2 6%	3 6%	0 ...	3 9%	2 6%	1 3%	0 ...	
	C	5 9%	2 5%	1 3%	1 5%	4 11%	2 5%	1 3%	0 ...	
General agriculture affiliations	A	6 11%	9 25%	3 9%	2 9%	9 26%	2 5%	7 1%	2 14%	48 16%
	B	9 14%	9 27%	7 15%	3 12%	8 24%	3 8%	6 18%	1 6%	
	C	7 12%	10 24%	5 14%	3 14%	9 26%	3 6%	7 20%	1 7%	
Total	A	10 19%	10 28%	3 9%	2 9%	12 35%	3 8%	8 24%	2 14%	58 19%
	B	12 18%	11 33%	7 15%	3 12%	11 33%	4 11%	7 21%	1 6%	
	C	11 20%	11 27%	5 14%	3 14%	12 34%	4 9%	8 22%	1 7%	
Times elected (average)	A	4.3	4.1	4.3	5.2	5.4	4.7	4.7	4.9	4.6
	B	4.1	4.2	4.4	5.7	5.4	4.9	4.9	4.4	
	C	4.3	4.2	4.3	5.4	5.4	4.7	4.7	4.5	
Year of birth (average)	A	1901	1905	1902	1901	1901	1900	1901	1898	1901
	B	1901	1905	1902	1902	1901	1901	1901	1898	
	C	1901	1905	1901	1901	1901	1901	1902	1897	

Sources: A, *Yomiuri Shimbun*; B, *Tōkyō Shimbun*; C, Watanabe, *Habatsu*.

ᵃ The totals factor out those having double designations, hence do not represent the addition of the two preceding columns.

ᵇ Including 15 persons who studied abroad.

Chart 13.   SOCIALIST PARTY FACTIONS AND THEIR SOCIOECONOMIC COMPOSITION.

(In number of members and percentage distribution)

Composition		Nishio		Kawakami		Suzuki		Wada		Matsumoto		Nomizo		Kuroda		Total	
Number of members	A	12	100%	51	100%	51	100%	17	100%	13	100%	5	100%	6	100%	168	
	B	27	100%	29	100%	39	100%	29	100%	12	100%	5	100%	6	100%	167	
	C	35	100%	32	100%	39	100%	30	100%	14	100%	4	100%	6	100%		
Ex-officials	A	6	8%	2	4%	2	4%	1	6%	0	...	0	...	0	...	7	(4%)
	B	11	4%	2	7%	2	5%	1	3%	0	...	0	...	0	...		
	C	1	3%	3	9%	2	5%	1	3%	0	...			0	...		
Ex-prefectural assemblymen	A	4	33%	18	35%	10	20%	5	29%	2	15%	2	40%	2	33%	45	27%
	B	7	26%	12	41%	9	23%	7	24%	1	8%	2	40%	1	17%		
	C	10	29%	12	38%	8	21%	7	23%	2	14%	2	50%	2	33%		
Ex-elected local officials	A	4	33%	17	33%	10	20%	5	29%	4	31%	2	40%	2	33%	49	29%
	B	9	33%	10	34%	9	23%	7	24%	3	25%	3	60%	2	33%		
	C	9	26%	14	44%	9	23%	7	23%	3	21%	2	50%	2	33%		
Total	A	6	50%	25	49%	16	31%	8	47%	4	31%	3	60%	3	50%	70	41%
	B	12	44%	15	52%	14	36%	11	38%	3	25%	3	60%	2	33%		
	C	15	43%	18	56%	13	33%	11	37%	4	29%	2	50%	3	50%		
Graduates of national or public universities or colleges	A	1	8%	16	31%	9	18%	7	41%	4	31%	1	20%	3	50%	49	30%
	B	4	15%	10	34%	8	21%	6	21%	6	50%	1	20%	3	50%		
	C	9	26%	10	31%	6	15%	10	33%	5	36%	1	25%	2	33%		
Graduates of private universities or colleges	A	2	17%	22	43%	12	24%	6	35%	6	46%	2	40%	1	17%	54	32%[a]
	B	7	26%	13	45%	7	18%	12	41%	5	42%	2	40%	1	17%		
	C	10	29%	14	44%	7	18%	12	40%	7	50%	1	25%	2	33%		
Business presidents, auditors, and members of boards of directors	A	1	8%	12	24%	4	8%	5	29%	2	15%	0	...	0	...	26	14%
	B	6	22%	4	14%	4	10%	5	17%	2	17%	0	...	0	...		
	C	6	17%	8	25%	3	8%	6	20%	2	14%	0	...	0	...		
General business affiliations	A	0	...	4	8%	3	6%	2	12%	0	...	0	...	0	...	10	6%
	B	1	4%	3	10%	4	10%	1	3%	1	8%	0	...	0	...		
	C	1	3%	3	9%	1	3%	3	10%	1	7%	0	...	0	...		

Chart 13.   (Continued)

Composition		Nishio	Kawakami	Suzuki	Wada	Matsumoto	Nomizo	Kuroda	Total
Total	A	1 8%	13 25%	7 14%	6 35%	2 15%	0 ...	0 ...	31 (18%)
	B	6 22%	5 17%	7 18%	6 21%	2 17%	0 ...	0 ...	
	C	6 17%	9 28%	4 10%	8 27%	2 14%	0 ...	0 ...	
Agricultural Coöperative Association leaders	A	1 8%	6 12%	2 4%	2 12%	1 8%	1 20%	0 ...	14 (8%)
	B	1 4%	3 10%	1 3%	3 10%	1 8%	1 20%	0 ...	
	C	3 9%	5 19%	4 10%	2 7%	0 ...	0	0	
Agricultural affiliations	A	0 ...	3 6%	0 ...	0 ...	1 8%	0	0	4 (2%)
	B	1 4%	1 3%	0 ...	0 ...	1 8%	0	0	
	C	1 3%	0 ...	1 ...	0 ...	1 7%	0	0	
Total	A	1 ...	8 16%	2 4%	2 12%	2 15%	1 20%	0 ...	17 (10%)
	B	2 17%	3 10%	1 3%	3 10%	2 17%	1 20%	0 ...	
	C	4 11%	5 19%	4 10%	2 7%	1 7%	0 ...	0 ...	
Labor union leaders and affiliated members	A	5 42%	8 16%	26 51%	5 29%	4 31%	0 ...	3 50%	55 (33%)
	B	10 37%	5 17%	17 44%	16 55%	3 25%	0 ...	3 50%	
	C	11 31%	3 9%	18 46%	12 40%	5 36%	0 ...	3 50%	
Farmer union leaders and affiliated members	A	2 17%	10 20%	7 14%	3 17%	2 15%	5 100%	2 33%	33 (20%)
	B	4 15%	7 24%	6 15%	4 14%	1 8%	5 100%	2 33%	
	C	5 14%	7 22%	7 18%	5 17%	2 14%	4 100%	2 33%	
Total	A	6 50%	18 35%	31 61%	9 53%	6 46%	5 100%	5 83%	84 (50%)
	B	12 44%	11 38%	22 56%	20 69%	4 33%	5 100%	5 83%	
	C	13 37%	11 34%	24 62%	16 53%	7 50%	4 100%	5 83%	
Times elected (average)	A	5.5	4.2	3.3	3.8	3.4	3.2	6.6	3.8
	B	4.2	4.4	3.4	3.2	4.1	3.2	6.6	
	C	4.2	4.4	3.4	2.9	3.7	3.8	6.6	
Year of birth (average)	A	1900	1904	1908	1909	1906	1907	1903	1906
	B	1904	1903	1906	1910	1906	1907	1903	
	C	1905	1903	1906	1909	1907	1908	1903	

Sources: A, *Yomiuri Shimbun*; B, *Tōkyō Shimbun*; C, anonymous. In *C* the Nishio column is really the Democratic Socialist party.
a Including three persons who studied abroad.

Appendix

Chart 14.   RELATION OF SOCIALIST MEMBERS (BY FACTION)
WITH THE ORGANIZED LABOR MOVEMENT

(In numbers of members and percentage distribution)

	Nishio (Democratic Socialists)	Kawakami		Suzuki		Wada		Matsumoto		Kuroda		Nomizo		Total
A	12 seats	51		51		17		13		6		5		
B	27	29		39		29		12		6		5		168ᵃ
Cᵇ	35	32		39		30		14		6		4		
Xᶜ														
A	7 58%	16	31%	11	22%	0 ...		2	15%	2	33%	2	40%	42
B	10 37%	12	42%	10	26%	2	7%	1	8%	2	33%	2	40%	25%
C	11 31%	13	41%	12	31%	0 ...		2	14%	2	33%	1	25%	
Yᵈ														
A	0 ...	9	18%	24	47%	9	53%	3	23%	3	50%	3	60%	56
B	6 22%	5	17%	15	38%	18	62%	2	17%	3	50%	3	60%	33%
C	6 17%	5	16%	16	41%	16	53%	4	29%	3	50%	3	75%	
Zᵉ														
A	5 42%	25	49%	16	31%	8	47%	8	62%	1	17%	0 ...		70
B	12 41%	12	42%	14	36%	9	31%	9	75%	1	17%	0 ...		42%
C	18 51%	14	44%	11	28%	14	47%	8	57%	1	17%	0 ...		

Source: Compiled by us.

ᵃ Includes Independents not listed here.

ᵇ *C* = Democratic Socialists.

ᶜ X. Forty two seats. These members have had close connections with the prewar labor movement. Most of them were leaders of labor or farmer unions (and the prewar socialist parties) in the period between 1920–1940.

Occupational breakdown: Lawyers............. 7   Ex-elected local officials........ 2
                           Journalists........... 6   Farmer union leaders.......... 14
                           Physicians........... 2   Graduates of colleges.......... 21
                                                          Ex-prefectural assemblymen..... 22

ᵈ Y. Fifty six seats. These members joined the labor or farmer union movement after the war.

Occupational breakdown: Labor union leaders................ 39
                           (teachers' union, 11; national
                           railway, 6; private railway, 4)
                           Farmer union leaders.............. 17
                           Graduates of colleges.............. 27
                           Ex-prefectural assemblymen........ 15

ᵉ Z. Seventy seats. These members have not had experience in the prewar labor movements nor close connection with the postwar labor or farmer unions.

Occupational breakdown: Lawyers............. 12   Journalists................ 6
                           Ex-elected local   Business affiliated............. 17
                           officials........... 13   Graduates of colleges.......... 54
                           Physicians.......... 6   Ex-prefectural assemblymen..... 23

Appendix

Chart 15. PROFESSIONAL OCCUPATIONS REPRESENTED IN THE
HOUSE OF REPRESENTATIVES BY PARTY, 1947–1958

(In numbers of members and percentage distribution)

1947	Liberal Party		Democratic Party		Socialist Party	
	120		106		139	
Journalist	17	14%	9	8%	19	14%
Lawyer	15	13%	10	9%	16	12%
Teacher[a]	31	26%	20	19%	25	18%
Physician	1	...	0	...	1	...
Total	56	47%	37	35%	54	39%

1949	Democratic Liberal Party		Democratic Party		Socialist Party	
	261		75		46	
Journalist	36	14%	9	12%	3	7%
Lawyer	24	9%	4	5%	8	17%
Teacher	33	13%	11	15%	12	33%
Physician	1	...	0	...	1	...
Total	82	31%	23	31%	19	41%

1953	Liberal Party		Reform Party		(Right Wing) Socialist Party		(Left Wing) Socialist Party	
	237		76		66		71	
Journalist	36	15%	6	8%	10	15%	11	16%
Lawyer	27	11%	4	5%	15	23%	8	11%
Teacher	34	12%	10	13%	18	27%	11	16%
Physician	1	...	2	...	1	...	2	...
Total	85	36%	21	28%	35	53%	29	41%

1958	Liberal Democratic Party		Socialist Party	
	298		168	
Journalist	33	11%	18	11%
Lawyer	28	9%	19	11%
Teacher	31	10%	33	20%
Physician	2	...	8	5%
Total	88	30%	68	40%

Source: Compiled by us.

Note: It must be emphasized that this chart is not complete, nor does it provide the vital distinctions in such categories as "Journalist" or "Teacher."

[a] Mainly teachers and professors; also a considerable number of Teachers' Union leaders.

Appendix

Chart 16.　Percentage of Votes on a Party Basis in the 1958 House of Representatives Election

Basis	Liberal Democratic Party	Japan Socialist Party	Japan Communist Party	Minor Parties	Independents	Uncertain	Did Not Vote
Area:							
Six metropolitan centers	41	30	2	...	1	0	26
Other cities	56	25	0	...	2	2	15
Towns, villages	63	23	0	0	1	2	11
Sex:							
Male	60	26	1	0	2	1	10
Female	53	24	0	0	2	2	19
Age (male):							
20–24	43	41	1	...	1	...	14
25–29	45	39	3	...	1	3	9
30–39	54	35	1	0	1	1	7
40–49	63	25	0	...	1	2	9
50–59	72	16	0	...	2	2	8
60–over	72	10	...	...	4	1	13
Age (female):							
20–24	46	33	1	1	2	0	17
25–29	47	34	1	...	2	0	16
30–39	52	30	...	0	1	1	16
40–49	62	21	...	0	1	1	15
50–59	59	15	...	...	1	3	22
60–over	50	9	0	0	3	4	34
Occupation (male):							
Agriculture; forestry; fishing	70	19	0	0	2	0	9
Business; service; self-employed	75	15	1	...	2	1	6
Technical; white-collar	36	47	2	...	1	3	11
Labor	39	42	3	...	1	1	14
Occupation (female):							
Agriculture; forestry; fishing	61	17	0	0	2	2	18
Business; service; self-employed	58	20	0	0	2	2	18
Technical; white-collar	44	37	0	...	1	1	17
Labor	39	34	...	...	1	2	24
Education:							
New university; old higher and technical schools	51	33	2	...	2	3	9
Old middle school; new high school	55	31	0	0	1	1	12
Old high primary; new junior high	57	27	1	0	2	1	12
Primary school	58	15	...	0	2	2	23
Economic Class:							
Upper	77	16	...	...	...	...	7
Upper middle	61	23	1	1	2	2	10
Middle	55	27	1	0	1	1	15
Lower middle	50	25	0	0	2	2	21
Lower	55	17	...	...	4	2	22

Source: *Sōsenkyo no jittai* ("The Actual Conditions of the General Election"), Election Bureau, Local Autonomy Board, December, 1958, pp. 54–55.

Appendix

Chart 17. REASONS GIVEN BY VOTERS FOR SUPPORTING
A CANDIDATE IN THE 1958 HOUSE
OF REPRESENTATIVES ELECTION

Code	Number of Times Given as Additional Factor	Reason	Multiple Answers Permitted (per cent)		Answer Limited to Principal Reason (per cent)	
A	11	Liked his character	38	(45)ᵃ	23	(29)ᵃ
B	10	Support the party	29	(34)	16	(20)
C	3	Saw the brochure	28	(33)	8	(10)
D	12	Heard radio speech(es)	15	(18)	3	(4)
E	13	Saw newspaper advertisement(s)	15	(18)	2	(3)
F	1	Household conference	14	(17)	7	(8)
G	7	Heard public speech(es)	14	(17)	6	(7)
H	16	Because everyone said good things about him	7	(8)	3	(4)
I	14	Because I knew him well	6	(7)	3	(4)
J	2	Request from knowledge-able person	2	(3)	1	(1)
K	4	Advice from union or association	2	(3)	1	(1)
L	6	Advice from knowledge-able person	2	(2)	0	(0)
M	8	Message from candidate	2	(2)	1	(1)
N	5	Decision of town or hamlet	1	(1)	0	(0)
O	9	Because candidate is related to me	1	(1)	0	(0)
P	15	Because I am indebted to candidate	1	(2)	1	(1)
Q	. . .	Other	3	(4)	2	(3)
R	. . .	Don't know	5	(6)	3	(4)
		Total	185	(221)	80	(100)

Source: *Sōsenkyo no jittai*, pp. 59–60.

ᵃ Percentages in parentheses include those who did not vote.

Chart 18. BREAKDOWN OF REASONS GIVEN BY VOTERS FOR SUPPORTING A CANDIDATE IN THE 1958 HOUSE OF REPRESENTATIVES ELECTION—BY AREA, SEX, AGE, OCCUPATION, ECONOMIC CLASS, POLITICAL CONSCIOUSNESS SCALE, AND PARTY (Code letters supplied in Chart 17)

Basis	A	H	I-O-P	B	C	D	G	E	M	F	J-L	K	N	Q	R	Didn't Vote
Area:																
Six metropolitan cities	40	4	7	34	28	20	11	21	2	15	4	1	..	3	2	26
Other cities	39	8	7	30	26	12	16	13	1	13	5	3	0	3	5	15
Towns, villages	37	8	12	26	31	17	14	14	2	15	4	2	1	4	5	10
Sex:																
Male	43	5	10	38	33	18	19	17	2	8	3	3	1	3	3	10
Female	35	9	6	22	24	13	11	13	2	19	5	2	1	3	6	19
Age (male):																
20–24	37	7	5	42	37	18	24	22	1	8	3	1	..	2	4	14
25–29	35	3	9	42	35	14	21	9	2	4	3	8	..	..	3	9
30–39	42	3	5	44	34	16	16	22	2	7	1	4	2	4	2	7
40–49	48	4	9	39	36	24	21	21	2	8	4	2	1	2	1	9
50–59	48	9	14	34	35	18	20	16	1	8	5	3	..	4	3	8
60–over	41	6	15	28	25	16	12	10	2	9	3	1	2	4	5	13
Age (female):																
20–24	38	11	4	34	30	17	16	17	3	12	5	2	2	1	3	17
25–29	32	8	8	27	33	15	18	15	2	25	7	4	..	2	4	16
30–39	39	7	5	24	31	15	12	17	2	21	7	1	0	3	4	16
40–49	40	8	6	22	25	13	13	13	1	23	2	2	1	3	5	14
50–59	33	9	7	17	16	14	9	11	0	16	3	2	1	4	9	22
60–over	22	9	10	7	4	4	6	2	..	14	3	..	1	6	14	34
Occupation (male):																
Agriculture; forestry; fishing	42	8	13	34	36	19	15	17	3	8	4	1	1	4	3	9
Business; service; self-employed	47	4	10	40	29	19	24	15	1	9	3	1	0	3	1	6
Technical; white-collar	47	3	7	45	34	15	18	22	..	4	3	7	..	4	3	11
Labor	37	5	5	39	35	17	18	18	2	7	3	6	..	2	5	14

Chart 18. *(Continued)*

Basis	A	H	I-O-P	B	C	D	G	E	M	F	J-L	K	N	Q	R	Didn't Vote
Occupation (female):																
Agriculture; forestry; fishing	29	12	9	14	22	14	10	11	2	26	4	1	1	4	7	18
Business; service; self-employed	43	4	6	25	21	12	13	11	1	15	4	..	1	3	5	17
Technical; white-collar	39	6	5	33	33	17	15	17	2	14	4	5	0	1	4	17
Labor	32	12	4	23	24	11	6	16	1	18	4	2	1	4	7	24
Education:																
New University; old higher and Technical schools	42	3	6	52	32	13	22	18	1	7	3	5	..	5	1	10
Old middle school; new high school	41	4	10	37	32	16	16	18	1	11	5	3	0	3	2	12
Old high primary; new junior high	41	7	7	31	32	19	16	18	2	15	4	2	1	3	5	11
Primary school	30	10	9	15	18	9	9	7	1	17	3	1	0	4	7	24
Economic Class:																
Upper	42	3	17	41	24	15	21	15	2	13	6	2	..	2	4	8
Upper middle	43	5	12	34	32	18	16	18	2	11	4	2	1	4	3	10
Middle	38	7	7	30	28	16	15	14	2	15	4	2	1	3	5	15
Lower middle	34	11	4	20	24	13	11	13	0	15	4	2	0	3	7	21
Lower	26	9	6	10	28	9	12	15	1	13	2	..	..	3	12	22
By Political Consciousness Scale:[a]																
A	47	3	8	54	44	21	24	21	2	11	4	4	1	1	1	..
B	53	6	10	41	37	21	23	18	2	12	3	4	1	3	3	..
C	50	8	8	31	33	21	16	25	2	18	5	2	1	3	3	..
D	39	10	11	27	35	15	12	12	2	21	5	2	0	4	7	..
E	32	19	10	12	6	8	9	5	1	19	6	1	1	8	20	..
Party:																
Liberal Democratic	47	10	12	29	33	19	17	18	2	17	4	1	1	4	5	..
Japan Socialist	40	5	5	47	34	15	17	19	2	16	4	6	0	3	6	..

Source: *Sōsenkyo no jittai*, pp. 62–63.

[a] See p. 115.

INDEX

Agricultural Coöperative Association: as a potent pressure group, 67–68; cooperation extended by Liberal Democratic party, 84; most vital link for conservatives, 90; role in supporting conservative candidates, 91–92 and n. 11. *See also* agriculture

agriculture: importance as a pressure group after 1918, 15; effects of Occupation land reform, 26; unprecedented prosperity after 1949, 45; representation in party Diet membership, 67–69; "agrarian" population and voting strength, 90; Nōgyō Mondai Kenkyūkai ("Agricultural Problems Research Association") as central organ for agrarian interests, 91; voting rates in rural areas, 109. *See also* Agricultural Coöperative Association

Ashida Hitoshi: takes leadership in the immediate postwar period, 35; aligns with Katayama Tetsu, 40; becomes top political figure, 41

Association of Families Bereaved by the War, affiliated with the conservative party, 92

Bluntschli, Johann, affects early Meiji thought, 5

bureaucracy: in early Meiji era, 8–9; role of ex-officials in Meiji "popular parties," 10; "national interest" position of ex-officials, 12; "bureaucratization" of parties in party era, 13–15 and n. 5; conflict and coöperation with "pure politicans," 18; relative decline in numerical strength in the 1947 and 1949 elections, 35; increasing strength within conservative movement after 1949, 52; definition of ex-official, 55; close ties with business, 63–64; cleavage between "bureaucrats" and "pure politicians" within Liberal Democratic party, 74; influence of Liberal Democratic party on the local civil service, 93

Burke, Edmund, affects eary Meiji thought, 5

business: and Meiji officialdom, 8; mode of political participation in Meiji era, 11; conflict and coöperation with agriculture in party era, 18; intimate relations with postwar conservative parties, 63–66; Japanese business class and liberalism, 78; more extensive relations with Liberal Democratic party, 88–89. *See also* zaibatsu

cabinets: Katayama-Ashida and Ashida-Katayama cabinets undistinguished in performance, 37–38; important role of ex-officials after 1948, 57; university representation between 1948 and 1960, 61–62 n. 5; dominance of ex-officials after 1957, 74; opinion polls on Kishi, Hatoyama, Yoshida, and Ashida cabinets, 139 and n. 6; cause for resignation of Kishi cabinet, 141; selection of ministers in Ikeda cabinet, 143; composition of Kishi cabinet in June, 1959, 144 n. 9

Chōshū, supremacy in new Meiji government, 7–8

Communist party: establishment, 29–30; ideology, 31; in the 1946, 1947, and 1949 elections, 36; in the Diet elections between 1952 and 1960, 47–48; reasons for weakness, 50; affiliation of prefectural assemblymen and local council-

Index

Index